Lean Design in Healthcare

A Journey to Improve Quality and Process of Care

Lean Design in Healthcare

A Journey to Improve Quality and Process of Care

Adam Ward

Routledge
Taylor & Francis Group

LONDON AND NEW YORK

First published 2019 by Routledge

2 Park Square, Milton Park, Abingdon, Oxon OX14 4RN

605 Third Avenue, New York, NY 10017

Routledge is an imprint of the Taylor & Francis Group, an informa business

First issued in paperback 2021

ISBN-13: 978-1-138-49879-2 (hbk)
ISBN-13: 978-1-03-217859-2 (pbk)
DOI: 10.4324/9781351015554

Library of Congress Cataloging-in-Publication Data

Names: Ward, Adam (Adam Michael), author.
Title: Lean design in healthcare : a journey to improve quality and process of care / Adam Ward.
Description: Boca Raton : Taylor & Francis, 2018. | Includes bibliographical references and index.
Identifiers: LCCN 2018020481 (print) | LCCN 2018022123 (ebook) | ISBN 9781351015554 (e-Book) | ISBN 9781138498792 (hardback : alk. paper)
Subjects: | MESH: Quality Improvement | Delivery of Health Care--organization & administration | Total Quality Management | Efficiency, Organizational | Process Assessment (Health Care)--methods | United States
Classification: LCC RA971 (ebook) | LCC RA971 (print) | NLM W 84.4 AA1 | DDC 362.1068--dc23
LC record available at https://lccn.loc.gov/2018020481

I would like to dedicate this book to the following people:

My wife, Heather, for leading me on this journey when she entered healthcare before me and for putting up with my crazy travel and one million questions as I dove into learning the industry. You are the best!

My former CEO, Marc Hafer, for pushing me into healthcare and never letting me give up on finding a solution.

My boss, colleague, and close friend, John Gallagher, for dreaming with me and partnering with me as we tackled healthcare clients together.

My publisher, Kris Mednansky, for taking a conversation with me at her trade show booth and successfully turning it into a book.

Lastly, the real people of the Obeya 'Ohana who served as the inspiration for the characters of this book. You pushed me to be my best.

Contents

Foreword

If Innovation Is the Answer, Are You a Player or a Spectator?

"Innovation" is frequently offered as the "way out of the woods" for American healthcare. And why not? As Americans we are reminded of the power of innovation to reshape our world many times a day as we tap on our cell phones to find our way through traffic to a place we have never been, purchase a new pair of shoes from an online retailer, or check out our friends on Facebook as we pass the time in the waiting room of a specialist to whom we have been referred. It's not just consumer electronics that demonstrates the power of innovation in our world. If you have ever flown on Southwest Airlines you know that it has transformed air travel with a new business model.

Much has been written about how healthcare is a contrary industry. The "invisible hand" of the market does not seem to be able to find the handle in healthcare that opens the door to lower prices, profitability, and consumer satisfaction. Financial incentives seem to raise costs without improving performance. Despite growing concerns about unsustainable financial burdens and growing workforce shortages that will cost many access to care even as hospitals are shuttered, practices vanish, and many doctors and nurses are driven to early retirement or alternative careers, innovation does not seem to be able to save our day or bring a new day as it has in so many other industries.

Some say that innovation requires substantial resources and a larger enterprise. The rationale that a larger organization will be able to "innovate" has been frequently offered to regulators as justification for mergers that create virtual regional monopolies in healthcare in many markets. I am unaware of any of these promises that have yielded much fruit although I am aware that some large systems like Kaiser, Cleveland Clinics, University of Pittsburgh Medical Center (UPMC), and Geisinger have been more innovative than others.

Is innovation too expensive for most organizations to attempt or sustain? Is there a shortage of talent or creativity? Is today's workload too heavy to allow most organizations to look beyond the moment toward a future accessible only through innovation? Should innovation be left to groups of bright young engineers and entrepreneurs who will ship out solutions to all of our problems from Silicon Valley? Does innovation in healthcare fail because leading innovation requires a mindset not found in most healthcare executives? Do the "internal politics" of stressed organizations preclude innovation? All these and many other questions come up in Adam Ward's new book *Lean Design in Healthcare: A Journey to Improve Quality and Patient Care*.

Do we need a new book on innovation in healthcare? To answer that question I recently employed the innovation that has made going to the library a rare activity for me. I went to Amazon and typed in various configurations of phrases like "Healthcare Innovation." My "research" produced 15 books written since 2010. Titles such as *Innovation and Entrepreneurship in the Healthcare Sector: From Idea to Funding to Launch (2011)* and the more recent *Managing Innovation in Healthcare (2016)* were intriguing, as was *Before Disrupting Healthcare: What Innovators Need to Know (2016)*. Surely it would be a good idea to buy *Innovation the Cleveland Clinic Way: Powering Transformation by Putting Ideas to Work*. There are many options but none seemed appealing and the books themselves would probably be rather dry and technical and amount to yet another barrier for a busy leader or management team that had come to the conclusion that they must become innovative. It is barriers like that that keep consultants employed. Unfortunately, just hiring any consultant does not guarantee much more success than buying a boring book.

I have always been drawn to stories, and early in my tenure as a CEO I was delighted to discover Patrick Lencioni's little gem, *The Five Dysfunctions of a Team: A Leadership Fable*. After reading the "fable" I gave a copy of the book to everyone on my leadership team. Later on I discovered John Kotter and Lorne Whitehead's little book, *Buy-In: Saving Your Good Ideas From Being Shot Down*, another "fable" pregnant with great advice. Just last year I wrote the preface to another healthcare fable, *The Patient Centered Value System: Transforming Healthcare through Co-Design* by Anthony DiGioia, MD and Eve Shapiro. I hope that is enough proof to establish that I really like "how-to" books that use narratives to help the reader absorb information that is experiential but is denied to them because they have not "had the experience of…" To my list of favorite books that offer difficult to acquire wisdom and knowledge through "experiential" fables I will now add *Lean Design in Healthcare.*

The subject of innovation is complex, and there is no settled or widely accepted set of practices. As the story implies, there are experienced "gurus" or coaches who have received knowledge from other wise ones and often been part of the practiced art in industries that live or die on the ability of teams to constantly develop products that attract and delight customers. Adam Ward has such a background. He worked for many years for Honda and GE before he brought established industry concepts of innovation, which he personalized and advanced through his own experience, to healthcare.

One of my most positive experiences as a CEO was being part of the introduction of Lean to Atrius Health. As we got into the work of improving existing systems of care with Lean, it was easy to see that what we were doing was similar to what audio engineers were doing in the dying days of analog recording. You could wrestle incremental improvements from the old way of doing things, but what was really needed were innovations that enabled more portable and widely available devices for both recording and enjoying music. Once the shift was underway it did not take long for my old turntable to be moved to the attic. Our early work with Lean led me and others in our practice to realize that "running faster and more efficiently" was a move in the right direction, but it was time to begin to think about a whole new ballgame. Healthcare transformation meant redesign with bold objectives as the goal. Near the end of the book there is a conversation between two of the characters that captures part of the concern that made the need to develop our own innovative skills seem so important to me:

"Patients don't always want the next available appointment, they want the appointment when it works best for them."

"Our doctors' panels average 2,000 patients. We are pushing them to increase that number to 5,000 with our goal set at 10,000. There won't be enough physicians in the future to keep panel sizes low," Georgina explained.

"Even now, giving the patient the time most convenient for them is difficult. When we double or triple the number of patients for each doc, we have to focus on who sees the actual doc and who doesn't need to," Hoggs added.

The story demonstrates how vulnerable the idea of setting up a systematic approach to innovation will be to potential failure. It is not an overnight process and in organizations that are dominated by "operations" with leaders desperate to have results that are obvious within the next quarter there is little chance for success. It would be nice to think that good leadership would guarantee success, but that is not the story that is told. There are many subplots of misunderstanding, resistance from senior executives with alternative strategies, and just the hard work of team building in an environment where there is all the volatility, uncertainty, complexity, and ambiguity in an industry under attack for its failure to produce a sustainably affordable service for everyone. There were moments in the story when the lines of Rudyard Kipling's famous poem "If" seemed to be playing in the background:

If you can keep your head when all about you
Are losing theirs and blaming it on you...

Not to be a spoiler, but at the end of the fable there is still uncertainty. It is a real story. What is accomplished is that a team has been created. The innovation team, the CEO, and probably most of the surviving management team have learned that innovation is the product of intense curiosity that requires thousands of hours of inquiry and research with potential customers. It is not a solo act. Its success is grounded in the patience required to try and try again. They have learned that a guide that can coach, mentor, and encourage them to be patient and trust one another is an essential catalyst. If the team stays together, and if ripples of understanding of the process can begin to create understanding in the larger organization while expectations of miracles are managed along with those who would go another way that offers an easier path that is a blind alley, then there is hope.

Preface

I've been an innovator my whole life. From my first set of Legos to my latest client engagement, from personal life to professional, my viewpoint has always been that there is better. My foray into healthcare began a dozen years ago, following a dozen years designing cars for a world-class automaker.

The CEO of the Lean Transformation Consultancy I began working for pushed me to apply my expertise in healthcare delivery. I pushed back. He pushed harder, knowing that the industry was in desperate need of what we were doing.

After years of "experiments" with a host of clients, it clicked. If healthcare was going to do Lean Design, they needed a model that worked for them. They didn't need to drag in decades of project management practices that had been obsolete nearly as long. We also didn't want to grab the latest methodology, just because everyone else was talking about it or trying to do it.

That forced us to find the best of the best. I had countless debates with a multitude of practitioners across several industries. Objectivity to real-world performance, not theory, was king. Ultimately, we chose the best from each, customizing a package for nascent healthcare innovators.

The work we delivered wasn't about billable hours; it was about achieving results for clients. There was our pride in having an approach that was world-class, that could actually be adopted by healthcare, and that would produce repeatable, systemic innovation.

A lot of the principles, techniques and tools in this book can be read elsewhere. Some will argue subtleties or possibly everything. I'm not speaking from theory, but from the battlefield of the real world. Scars and successes. Few have studied the practical application of multiple methodologies in any industry, let alone healthcare delivery.

Finally, we're in the later stages of the digital transformation. The oldest working generation has reluctantly transitioned from a completely analog world and the youngest generation has known nothing but digital. Software is taking over. We're in real danger of losing a lifetime of process best practices because "being digital" is the silver bullet to fix everything. However, it can only enable fixes, not be the fixes. Process is irreplaceable. It transcends technology. We must learn from those who have gone before us and harness the energy and passion of those who are next.

This book is an allegorical compendium of the good and the bad, what works and what doesn't. It is all of my client experiences wrapped into one, with a major dose of one highly successful client. You will read about failures and successes. You will read insights into how to do Lean Design.

If you're in healthcare delivery and you need innovation, I challenge you to find a better recipe to start with. What are written in these pages are seeds to grow your own skills. The only decision is your level of implementation and your commitment to it. I've seen it done well. You can do it too. Read it, learn it, experiment with it and grow from it.

Adam Ward

Author

Adam Ward has nearly twenty-five years of innovation experience.

He worked at Honda R&D and GE Healthcare, honing his craft. At Honda he was known for his precision in maintaining cost, schedule and driving differentiation for his projects. During his time at GE, he helped institute the Chief Engineer Model, the Project Business Case, reBranding DI, and the Disruptive Cost Workout.

At Simper, an IBM company, he served dozens of clients across several industries. He served as the innovation subject matter expert, creating the strategy and content for client delivery. His vast experience across industries brings a breadth of knowledge to help lead client projects and transformations.

However, his focus on being an early pioneer with innovation techniques in healthcare delivery is what has really set Adam apart. He is as comfortable talking to healthcare executives as working in the trenches with doctors, nurses, and staff members. He has led patient care model redesigns of multiple healthcare clients for high-risk patients, the elderly, and internal medicine.

Adam has a Bachelor's Degree in Mechanical Engineering from the University of Maryland and an MBA from The Ohio State University. He guest lectures at Ohio State for both graduate and undergraduate programs.

He is a speaker and consultant on the topic of innovation.

Chapter 1

The Players

Marc removed his glasses and set them on the table. There were nearly twenty people in the room, but you could have heard a pin drop. A team of five was anxiously awaiting his feedback as their CEO, the CEO of Angstrom Health.

It had been a tough eighteen months for them. Although it was technically an experiment, Georgina considered it her life. Regardless of what the boss at the end of the table would say, she knew her team had done everything in its power to be successful. It was indeed a risk. As part of a large, physician-run healthcare system, this would stand as a critical moment in its history. She believed the data. She also knew it was intuitively correct.

It was clearly better for the patient. Their satisfaction scores were the highest they'd ever been in recent years. There was no arguing the health count outcomes either. They were simply better than even their best physician had previously achieved. While reimbursements were slightly less, the cost to deliver care was also down.

The problem was decades of tradition. Their team had just presented a completely new service line requiring virtually no doctors, and patients would not be seen in their traditional clinics, buildings with remaining, multi-year leases. On top of that, operating hours were radically different, aligning with peak patient times, not classic banking hours. It was dissimilar to anything they had done before. None of their competitors were doing anything even remotely similar.

She was also conscious about the amount of money that she had spent. It was a fairly significant amount and if the executive leadership team was displeased, this would probably be the end of her employment.

Marc was a great leader. A specialist, he had a storied, thirty-five-year career. He still practiced, albeit just a day a week. The entire Executive Leadership Team (ELT) respected him. Success had followed him his whole life. He had played college football at a Division I school and had run marathons for years, ultimately setting a personal record of 2:30. His network was massive, a result of years of cordially engaging with others. With a near photographic memory, he could recall facts about everything: medicine, history, sports, philosophy and more.

There would possibly be some debate on issues, but the ELT would follow whatever he ultimately decided.

"When you first brought me the initial proposal," Marc said, "I made a statement. I told you that I had never seen the data presented as your team had done. It was the story you told from that data that sold me on funding this experiment." Marc folded his hands in front of him and chose his next words carefully. Georgina's team members were struggling not to smile, but one young man was showing all of his teeth in a giant, goofy grin. The leader remained stoic, not wanting to celebrate early.

"But a lot has changed in the past year and a half. Regulatory uncertainty, physician burnout and declining reimbursements have put extreme pressure on our organization."

The executives around the table nodded in agreement. She looked at each of them. Right next to Marc was Richard Mann, the CFO.

Financial

Richard Mann was one of the few executives who didn't have a background in medicine. He was all about the numbers. A former consultant, he had been brought on board years ago to help Marc lead the turnaround from near bankruptcy. Richard knew what he was doing. He had trained the entire organization in how Angstrom Health made money. He was amazed how few executives and even fewer physicians knew how money flowed in healthcare. Admittedly, it was complex, far more so here than in virtually every other nation on earth, but it was a product of the American culture it was birthed in. There were three powerful parties. The most powerful was the government, which set reimbursement rates for half of all Americans, those on Medicare and Medicaid, the military and VA and a handful of others. Next powerful were payers, the insurance companies who were clearly making more profit than health systems, under pressure to do so as publicly traded companies. They had money and they lobbied hard with it. They controlled the insurance premium dollar. They collected the money and disbursed it. Everyone with private insurance, all working America, was a captive in their prison of rules. It seemed they loved to deny claims. The entire billing process had become so convoluted that health systems paid third-party firms millions of dollars to manage their revenue cycle, hoping to get back a slightly higher fraction of what they deserved for the care they provided.

Georgina remembered her conversation with the coach about the revenue cycle. That term was made up for healthcare. Other industries didn't have it. Somehow, the triangle of policy, payer and provider made it extremely difficult to get paid for the care delivered. Meanwhile pharmaceuticals and medical device companies were getting exactly what they were charging, at the expense of the health systems. It was capitalism on the insurance premium dollar. Everyone agreed with Richard on this point: Payers were the necessary evil that healthcare systems were forced to work alongside. The third group, providers, could seem at times, overly altruistic.

"Providers" included all healthcare systems, hospitals, clinics and ancillary locations. It included anyone who delivered healthcare to a patient. They were powerful because they were the only ones who could deliver care. Without them, there was no healthcare. Ultimately, outside of the fifty percent of spend, the government made policy and payers were the bank. Healthcare could exist without them. Historically, it had. But these were difficult days. In other countries, the government ran everything, with exceptions where providers were independent. Healthcare had become politically contentious. Richard didn't have a position on whether the Affordable Care Act (ACA) should be replaced or not. He just wanted to know how Angstrom Health would get paid for the work they delivered. The uncertainty of the market was annoying, particularly given the colossal momentum of the industry. Turning like a battleship would be an improvement. This was one of the slowest industries to make and adopt changes, no doubt due to the tension between the three players. Financial changes had an instant ripple effect. They had large investments in buildings and equipment. Then there was the highly specialized and expensive payroll. Decisions regarding those took years to plan and deliver. As a non-profit, they managed a razor-thin margin of just a couple percent. Small fluctuations made a big impact. They had survived state healthcare overhaul and were figuring out how to deal with the ACA. He hadn't quite figured that out. The country was spending 18% of its gross domestic product (GDP), about $10,000 per person per year, on healthcare, yet providers were financially struggling.

Somewhere in the mix was the patient, who directed the dollars by choosing where to get care. A few years ago, there was a significant number of patients who didn't have insurance. That hurt financially. It required large write-offs each year. Worse, it filled precious moneymaking appointments with patients who couldn't pay. Fortunately, that wasn't the case anymore. His state had required its citizens to have insurance years before the nation followed with the ACA and then the individual mandate repeal. To Georgina, all Richard ever cared about was the number of relative value units (RVU) and average length of stay (LOS) in the hospital. The more RVUs, the better. Margin and cash on hand were more important than anything else. With a higher number of RVUs, the organization earned more revenue. As for LOS, the lower the better. Get people treated and get them out with no complications, was Richard's opinion. Reimbursement was fixed for most people being treated as inpatient, a typical result for their stage in life. Heaven forbid we have a readmit. "But at what expense?" Georgina often thought. "That is easier said than done." They were penalized on reimbursements based on their patients' readmission rate and timing. "We can't just kick them out early and hope they're OK," Georgina told herself constantly.

A focus on RVUs and LOS as the primary success metrics drove an entire set of behaviors that Georgina had grown to loathe. It was bad for everybody, from physicians to patients. It was a game that finance played with insurance. It may have helped regarding insurance contracts but it provided no indication of how good the delivered care was. It forced physicians to rush. Rushing led to less time with patients and less focus on their overall health, as opposed to merely the chief complaint presented at their most recent appointment.

Richard was the most difficult ELT member to deal with. "He's just so nearsighted," Georgina thought. This man hated to invest in anything without an immediate payback. It appeared that he had no vision whatsoever. To Richard, Georgina and her team of innovators were a thorn in his side. He couldn't manage the morass of the current system, let alone plan for an uncertain future. He certainly didn't need to deal with her crazy ideas of disruption. The organization wasn't flexible enough for that. Marc knew they were both right. That's why he forced the two to cooperate on solutions. The pace of change had to be right. Too fast, and the savings wouldn't cover the current investments on top of the new ones. Too slow, and they risked facing financial failure for being obsolete, getting disrupted from outside of the industry. Retail clinics were a prime example of this. They had a cost and convenience advantage Angstrom Health couldn't match.

They were doing stuffy noses now, but how long before they were treating chronic diseases? Richard was focused on their traditional competitors, other giant health systems, but disruptors were what kept Marc up at night. Georgina knew that. In fact, she was partially responsible for it. The early data her team had provided, which Marc had just referenced, was a State of the Union of sorts for Angstrom Health. It was a complete analysis of their system and market. The alarming conclusions had helped get her team fully funded. She just hoped what they had done since would keep them going. Richard was a wild card.

Operations

Next to Richard was Jill, the Chief Operating Officer. "She is one tough woman," Georgina reflected. "My kind of woman, actually."

Initially a vocal opponent of the work, Jill had become an ally, one of Georgina's biggest supporters. The two had had some difficult conversations, some heated arguments and some impasses that felt congressional, neither side budging, each passionately representing their stakeholders. There was a lot of irony in that. Representing their stakeholders. They were on the same team. They both wanted to deliver excellent care and keep Angstrom Health independent.

Despite not being a physician, Jill probably had the most initials behind her name. She started as an Orthopedic Nurse Practitioner with a PhD, serving as an officer in the U.S. Army. It was intense work, taking care of soldiers with war injuries. Her Masters of Public Health was earned during her time in the military and her MBA immediately afterward. Jill had specialty certifications in what seemed like a dozen areas. She was well versed in all things healthcare and was invited regularly to speak at conferences. Nothing seemed to faze her, except stupidity.

There was no tolerance for incompetence. Georgina recalled one meeting where Jill said, "You know that saying, 'There are no stupid questions, just stupid answers?' Well, that's not true. That question you just asked," she continued, addressing another colleague in the meeting, "was the dumbest thing I've ever heard. Do your research before you say stuff like that. You're embarrassing yourself."

Jill wasn't wrong. The executive who was the target of that tirade no longer worked there. To Georgina's recollection, Marc had fired him just a few weeks later.

"Or did he resign?" Georgina wondered. It didn't matter. His termination had been a long time coming. That type of public humiliation wasn't typical in healthcare, with most people opting for the far less obvious passive-aggressive route. Nothing could be proven that way. Jill didn't have time for that. She had to get stuff done. Everyone on her team liked that. Issues were discussed and resolved in the open, much like what Georgina did with her team. There were few things that destroyed a team as fast as a mutiny. Fortunately, Georgina was extremely intelligent and Jill respected that. It didn't keep those two from taking vastly different sides on issues.

Pride was often the thing that kept people from considering another solution, especially after making a public statement. Public here meant a statement to the ELT. The issue was no longer about what was best, it was about saving face. Both Jill and Georgina had to kowtow to the greater good, what was best for the system and what was best for the patient. As the COO, Jill held the highest day-to-day responsibility for delivering business results. Indeed, some felt Jill would take over when Marc eventually decided to retire. She may not have the relationship with Marc that Richard did, but she held far more responsibility. There were thousands of people under her organization chart, nearly 80% of the entire workforce. That didn't matter. Whatever metrics Richard was pushing, she had to provide. For the past few years, it had been increasing RVUs and reducing LOS. This had often put her at odds with Georgina's ideas. However, Jill knew they would have to move the ship in the direction Georgina was pushing. She just didn't know how fast they could move that way.

Medical

Dr. Steve Bertram, the Chief Medical Officer, was another story. Georgina wasn't sure what his position was. Two years into his role, he was still establishing his own feel toward his area of responsibility. There were hundreds of providers under him. He obsessed over what his physicians thought. Sometimes, his ideas for what should be done were just crazy. He was a pediatric oncologist and constantly fought for whatever would help the patient. Adults and less-funded areas of medicine were new to him in this role. Money and treatment plans were rarely an issue for him. He had been in long enough to know what his direct reports and medical team thought. He was an avid learner, and Georgina thought that maybe he read too much. He had shown both extreme pleasure and displeasure at her team's work. If it made his physicians happy, he was all for it. However, if even a couple of his prominent physicians didn't like it, he let Georgina know. He often floated technological solutions for his staff to Georgina, hoping she would help him get some of them implemented. They had worked on a couple together. Implementing a technology was one of the easier things her team did. However, it required a little bit of investigation.

One of the things that kept Dr. Bertram up at night was the idea of shifting to risk-based care. All he and his staff had ever known was episodic, fee-for-service delivery. In the past year, the system had hired a VP for Population Health that reported to him. For now, they were just focused on identifying and stratifying patients according to risk, but he knew that they would have to have a fully longitudinal look at the patients' lives. It was the only way that they could monitor health outcomes to minimize the amount of acute exacerbations from chronic diseases and any related hospitalizations. In a risk-based environment, that was money out the window. However, it required a tight relationship with the patient and more than the traditional annual physical in the amount of interaction. He didn't know how they would do it. They were talking about some type of electronic communication between provider and patient, but it was hard enough just trying to get through the number of daily appointments that were scheduled. He had no idea how they were going to be proactive and engage the patient outside of scheduled appointments. Perhaps they would later acquire another technology that would help.

In another career, this guy could've been a CIO—ironically, the person who sat directly to his left. The two were close and relied heavily on technological advances for competitive differentiation.

Informatics

Joe Christov, the Chief Information Officer (CIO) was a former electronic medical record (EMR) vendor developer. He was a great acquisition by the new head of HR. In just a few months, he had fixed some major issues and begun consolidation onto a single EMR platform for both ambulatory and inpatient settings. Joe was responsible for more than the EMR. He was responsible for the entire informatics infrastructure, including all related software and hardware. There were some gray areas between Joe, Jill and Dr. Bertram. Vendors didn't help. They were blurring the responsible department boundaries of their solutions and each of the three wanted to maintain control of their respective areas.

Joe was supportive of Georgina's effort but was constantly distracted by operational issues, upgrades and rollouts. Richard wanted to downsize Joe's organization while Joe was asking for nearly a doubling of FTEs, presumably for expanded capabilities. The two rarely agreed on anything, often loudly debating, but still keeping things professional.

Georgina's team had helped Joe's team develop a Robotic Process Automation (RPA) solution for their biggest manpower drain, password resets. The performance excellence (PE) team had conducted a value stream analysis (VSA) of the process, getting good results with a 20% reduction, but it was the RPA that got Joe to believe in Georgina's team. It had cut his team's involvement in password resetting by 70%, freeing up resources to do more important things.

Joe was concerned about getting ahead of the curve regarding artificial intelligence and precision medicine. These were areas Joe and Dr. Bertram had been discussing to maintain competitive advantage. Georgina warned them against adopting the latest techniques simply because they were available. They needed to be adopted in the context of their organization and with Angstrom at the helm, not because a vendor pushed a product on them.

Vendors were savvy. They knew how to market their products. The technologies were often impressive. The carefully crafted sales pitches often spoke of best-case potential. Big savings. Big improvements. Big advantages.

Big money, too. Georgina knew Joe had a massive budget. Most of it went to paying for the host of cybersolutions needed to run a health system. Despite the spend, they rarely did post-mortem reflections on performance relative to what was sold. It seemed that every year the vendors would come back, pushing their latest improvements and upgrades on the same value proposition they had initially used. They hadn't even stayed around long enough for Angstrom Health to get proficient on what they had sold them initially. It seemed like no time went by and they were looking for subscription extensions and new upgrades Angstrom had "passed on" with the first contract.

The problem with technology was that vendors rarely considered the overall workflow. Even the best suppliers would only consider their own technology's workflow. The new solution almost always increased effort, despite what they claimed. To their credit, it did provide them with additional information or insights or capability. But at what cost? Georgina was thinking about human cost, not direct spend. These tech solutions rarely made the job easier. Dr. Bertram knew this, but if a hotshot surgeon had asked for something, the work just got pushed down hill. Georgina felt it was her team's responsibility to ensure the solution was better overall. They had to stop buying the latest shiny object just because it was the latest shiny object.

Joe was a sucker for new capability. He loved it and he wanted it. It was like he was building the ultimate system for himself. Was this what CIOs talked about at conferences? Georgina thought back to high school when the computer nerds were discussing processor speed, amount of memory and hard drive size.

"Some things never change," she thought. "Just bigger toys."

Joe knew how to sell the spend to the ELT. He just played to the savings they could generate for Richard and what it would enable physicians to do for Dr. Bertram. United, the two of them could convince Marc of nearly anything. It was a triangle Georgina had to learn how to manage. Jill had refused to play their game, instead using brute force and positional power to get her way. Despite where society stood, Georgina was facing a boy's club and didn't have the title to push them around. She had to get in. Greasing the wheels of egos and being a social butterfly was not what she enjoyed. She saw it as a waste of her time. Fortunately, she had a team member who excelled interpersonally and made fellow females proud. She would gladly delegate the bulk of that effort to her.

Nursing

On the other side of the table was Valerie, the Chief Nursing Officer. She was ecstatic about the team's work. Strong, but soft-spoken, she had partnered with the team from the beginning. At times, it might have even been her encouragement that kept the team leader moving forward. Ironic that a nurse was encouraging a doctor.

Valerie had several layers of nurses she was responsible for, although she had no direct responsibility for any of them. They all reported up through operations. That just didn't make sense to her. It wasn't the case for physicians. Dr. Bertram had all of them under him. Nurses made up the single biggest line item for personnel spend. In fact, it was almost equivalent to what they spent on buildings and equipment. It was for this reason that every nurse reported up through their service lines to Jill. Without nursing, they were just a handful of support staff keeping things going. If operations were to succeed, Jill had to control nursing. Valerie didn't agree, but she didn't care enough to fight Jill on this one. She had enough to worry about keeping the nurses qualified and used to their best potential without being the dumping ground for the system.

Nurses ran everything. They did things those under them were too busy to do and whatever the docs felt like pushing on them. There were multiple layers of certification from nursing assistants (CNAs) to licensed practical nurses (LPNs), through registered nurses (RNs), to nurse practitioners (NPs). They could be additionally certified in specific specialties. Valerie held additions certification as an Oncology Certified Nurse (OCN). This helped with her relationship with Dr. Bertram. They had actually worked together a couple of times over their careers, but Valerie dealt with adults with cancer, not children, so it was limited to a couple of clinical trials that overlapped.

She desperately wanted more independence for her nurses. They were a magnet institution, recognized for their nursing excellence, and had highly capable nurses. By law they were allowed to do more than they did, especially her NPs, but they were constantly kept in check by the physicians. This had to change if she was going to help the careers of the existing nurses and continue to attract new ones.

Besides, there was no other employee that played as big a role in patient satisfaction as the nurse. They could calm an angry patient or exceed expectations with a simple act. The entire ELT knew this and gave Valerie a fairly large amount of latitude, as long as it kept Bertram's team happy.

Georgina knew there were other executives in the room, each running a valuable function of the business, but none played as crucial a role in determining her team's fate, and for that matter the organization's, as these did.

Marc went around the room and gave each of the ELT members a chance to share their thoughts. There were no big surprises for the team leader. They were in line with the private conversations she had held with each. There was one, an unexpected verbal dart, that caught her off guard, but not anything worse than what she'd experienced in the past.

"We're investing millions into your team. It's coming directly from our cash reserves. This must have a great ROI," Richard started. This wasn't the first time a team had asked to fund what Richard considered a non-essential activity. A few years ago, the PE team had been set up to do what seemed to him like the same thing.

"And I'm not talking cost avoidance," he continued. "That's hypothetical savings. I want real savings. We need what your team comes up with to lower our cost-to-deliver services. Expenses must drop. I expect at least a five- to ten-times return." Richard stopped talking.

"I'm going to echo Richard on the expense reduction," Jill took over with a stern voice. "However, it's more important to me that you don't anger the providers and staff. I can't afford the attrition. We're already estimating twenty percent of our providers hitting retirement age in the next seven to ten years. We need all of them to stay. It costs us about five hundred thousand to recruit and onboard one new doc. They need to be included on every project.

"Simultaneously, we need solutions to take into account the number of new graduates entering the workforce. That number is way down. There isn't enough supply to hit demand given our current care model. I don't know how to fix this but I hope you can. Otherwise, disruptive competitors might acquire us and we'll lose our valuable independence." She was finished.

It was Dr. Bertram's turn to talk. "Look, I know you guys are challenging everything. I have a team of docs that have been practicing for decades. They've seen and experienced everything. They are more dissatisfied than ever. Zero additional administrative burden. Help return the joy to medicine, not take it away. Tread carefully," he warned.

"However, we are committed to achieving better outcomes. If your team can demonstrably improve the health of our patient population, I will support you. Just make it easier for the doctor to do that, not harder."

Joe started talking almost immediately, as if finishing Dr. Bertram's statement. "Our infrastructure is complex. We're in the middle of an EMR consolidation. My team is taxed to the maximum. I can't have you asking for this feature or that software. We all have busy jobs and a strategic focus already."

He didn't say it out loud, but he might as well have. He hated others researching technology solutions. He had his own list of things he wanted to implement and any other effort took resources away from that.

"Are you handcuffing them before they start?" Jill fired back.

The room was silent for a moment following these comments. People looked at Marc. His face was free of expression. Joe didn't have the best social graces, but even he knew not to respond.

Valerie started to speak. "From everything I have seen and experienced, your team is improving the patient experience. My team is historically the most passionate about the patient."

The comment stung, but she was right. The ELT was mature and seasoned enough not to let it bother them. Dr. Bertram let it slide.

"We look forward to discovering what expanded roles and responsibilities we can be a part of," Valerie added.

They didn't have the longest hours, but nurses were the most abused roles in healthcare. They covered for those under them and took the undesirable jobs those more educated than them passed down. They were capable of doing much more, especially the Nurse Practitioners (NP), but physicians actively limited what they did. Why did NPs and Physicians have to engage in constant one-upmanship and questioning of each other's roles? Perhaps it was ego. Maybe it was fear of losing their job. It didn't matter. It was real. It was sad that there had to be such a competition. Several states, including their own, had passed regulations allowing a significant level of independence for NPs, but organizational momentum prevented them from taking on those roles.

Physicians claimed that NPs ordered more tests to make diagnoses. NPs claimed that their patient satisfaction scores were higher. Both had some data to back their claims up, but the truth was that NPs earned a fraction of the salary and more would be entering the job market in the near future. RNs were also underutilized. Valerie saw Georgina's team as an opportunity to demonstrate her nursing team's capabilities. She knew Jill did too. The org chart was unnecessarily complicated, surely as a result of this dynamic. Physicians were under the CMO. Nursing was technically under operations; however, Valerie was their medical leader. She had no positional authority but had to answer for all care related issues.

The room fell silent again. There were other ELT members who could comment. Certainly they had an opinion; however, the inner circle had spoken. There was no reason to muddy the water with another viewpoint.

"Maybe some of them don't need to be on the team any longer," Marc thought. He jotted a quick note to himself as a reminder to revisit this idea later.

The team stared intently at Marc as he looked up from his notebook.

Marc began to speak, "We're on the edge of a precipice. Our industry is facing major pressure. Every decision has big implications. With that being said, I have come to a conclusion about your project."

"That was the first time he had called it a project. He had always called it an experiment. What did that mean?" Georgina wondered.

"In all my years of medicine, I have never seen something so convincingly impressive," he stated matter-of-factly.

The team released a sigh, apparently having been holding their collective breath.

"It's so good that I believe every health system should do it. Everyone should have their version. I'm not referring to the new service line; that is equally amazing and will serve as the anchor for a string of new services your team will create."

She allowed the side of her mouth to curl upwards as Marc keep talking.

"We must expand and duplicate your entire process, culture, and approach. Our system will stand as a beacon for others, blazing the trail for true healthcare transformation. Healthcare can't wait for insurers or the government to decide what's right for our patients and our organization. Your approach gives us the capability to be flexible to whatever path they take us on. As long as we're making money, we're good. This will enable us to do that. In addition, we may actually be the first system to make significant improvements relative to the IHI Triple Aim."

Though a doctor, Marc hated referring to the Quadruple Aim. If they did things right, the physicians would be happy. The team's work stood as proof of that. Neither was he a fan of Accountable Care Organizations (ACO). His organization was one, but he had only reluctantly agreed to it. Although their scores were high and performance exemplary, he never felt its impact and financial returns were worth the effort.

"This may also be the first truly patient-centric effort I have ever seen. In the past, it has been lip service. We've used gimmicks and clever language to trick both us and our patients into thinking they're first, but we keep putting them through the same annoying process, catering to *our* needs. Who would have known you could fix both simultaneously?" he asked rhetorically.

This was way better than she had imagined. He must make a heck of a good poker player. He had been supportive during the entire process, but he had constantly challenged them, pushing back on their assumptions, and always wanting more. She hadn't been able to read him throughout today's presentation, and then get this reaction. She was elated.

"I need you to do three things. First, begin full operations of the new service line immediately. She'll give you all the support you need," he said, motioning toward Jill.

"Secondly, I expect you to create a full documentation of your process, from the initial idea until now. Include everything: technical details, interpersonal issues, things to consider and anything else pertinent. We need to provide a recipe others can follow."

Were they gonna sell their recipe or give it away? Her mind wandered for an instant before coming back. She couldn't be distracted. For now.

"Lastly, I want a new proposal for your team. Show me a structure where we can go faster. We need this everywhere and we need it now. HR will assist you and we'll find funding. Any questions?" he concluded.

She had a million, but didn't want to take up any more of the group's time. "I'm sure I will," she responded, "but for now I will get moving on what you requested. Thank you for your support and the support of the executive leadership team."

"You are dismissed," he said. He wasn't being literally dismissive; her team was merely the second-to-last item on day-long agenda for the executive leadership team as they prepped for their annual strategy retreat. The ELT applauded as the team left the room. It was a tradition Marc had started years ago, and it had stuck. Staff loved it.

When the door closed behind them, the team gave each other high fives, hugged each other, and quietly but energetically cheered.

"I'm so proud of all of you," Georgina said. "We took on something that seemed impossible and proved it could be done. Now it won't be what Mayo or Cleveland Clinic does. It will be what do *we* do."

The smiles were huge now. Several were laughing while others were crying tears of joy.

"We have a lot of hard work ahead of us. It isn't every day a healthcare system stands up an innovation center from scratch. In fact, there are just a few dozen. On top of that, we delivered results in record time," she said, during several more high fives between team members.

"We need to tell the world what we did and how we did it while simultaneously taking our own effort to the next level. For now, we celebrate! Tonight's dinner and drinks are on me! Where are we headed?"

Foundations

The celebration dinner at Little Kingston, a local ethnic restaurant, was dying down. The team liked to try new places to eat and foods from other countries. This in itself was a testament to their culture of change. They wouldn't be sucked in to the traditional steakhouse or chart house dinner. No, tonight they were eating Jamaican, if a slightly Americanized version of it. Most people were finishing a holiday sorrel or a ginger beer. A few enjoyed a cup of fresh roasted coffee.

"So what are we going to do tomorrow?" Sheryl blurted out during a rare pause in conversation.

Sheryl was the data analyst assigned to the team. Writing queries that summoned the electronic data warehouse to spit out the right information was a skill set that didn't necessarily translate to a high emotional intelligence level. Everybody was thinking about the question because they knew they had a significant amount of work, but no one wanted to ask. It had to be a lot and they just wanted to enjoy the win.

"First, I want you to take tomorrow off and enjoy a three-day weekend. Then we'll talk on Monday," Georgina told the team.

She took care of the bill and the team filed out the door together, walking toward their individual spots in the parking lot. Some would be taking a rideshare back to their place. After all, it was the convenient and responsible thing to do.

Georgina got into her all-wheel-drive SUV for the thirty-minute commute back to her house in the suburbs. She had had only one drink and that was an hour ago, so she was fine. Winters here could be tough, so all-wheel drive was necessary, especially for a healthcare worker. The ride gave her plenty of time to think about the meeting and reflect on the past eighteen months. It had exceeded her expectations. They had worked hard to get where they were, but she knew this was just the beginning. Doing something once was a much different story than documenting it for the world and then getting even better next time.

She wondered about where she would start. Although the project had started a year and a half ago, the effort to get where they were was a full thirty-six months in the making. It had begun as a single line item from an ELT strategy meeting. She'd never thought that it would take her where she was today. When she thought about everything, there were three distinct buckets: foundational basics, framework and the tools.

Chapter 2

The Basics

It seemed so long ago. Only a couple of years, but the progress and maturation of the team during that time was undeniable. Both Georgina and the team had gotten quite close to the expert during their journey. They simply referred to him as their coach, even though he was a consultant. Some of the senior executives loathed consultants. To tell the truth, the coach didn't like the term consultant either. It was often associated with unnecessary spending and mediocre results. He didn't want to be lumped in with that group of IT professionals or cost-cutters that healthcare workers had grown to hate. The ELT didn't like paying for consultants. Many wished they just would hire someone or develop existing employees.

Georgina thought about that for a moment. Just hire them or develop them. It was a very senior leadership thing to say, as if they could flip some switch and immediately have the capability in-house. Looking back now, that was one of the smartest decisions she had made, pushing back on that. She remembers talking to the coach about it. He wasn't pushy and didn't try to do a big sales job. The coach simply knew what worked and stated the facts. He wouldn't have held anything against her if she had chosen to reject his services, but he knew the journey would have been virtually impossible without him. She thought about her patients. There are very few people who can elevate their personal health all by themselves. The ones who get health coaches or a trainer or join a group with expertise have far better results. She couldn't force help on patients; they had to choose willingly. The times that someone had used the referral and engaged she counted among her proudest moments. She recalled fondly one patient who had dramatically changed his life.

"We *must* use a coach," Georgina told Marc and Richard. "We have no idea what we're doing and we have almost no existing ability among our staff."

She wasn't trying to be rude about the current employee base; they were just focusing on day-to-day operations. There were standouts that like to think about the future and radical improvement. She knew that she would have to pull them in, but she needed access to somebody who had made it their career to do exactly this.

"It's a lot of money," Richard countered, "to spend on just one person."

"Yes, if you look at the rate, it is. However, if you look where we need to go, we want the highest probability of success," Georgina calmly stated.

"Can you just research other places that have done this or read some books or articles?"

"You mean, like the ones I give my out-of-shape patients?"

Richard looked down at his gut, which hung well over his belt. He knew that wasn't a personal attack but he couldn't help feeling a little sting from it. She was right. He had been given all kinds of brochures and literature to read. He was surrounded by healthcare professionals daily. Yet here he was, in his late forties and out of shape. His father had only made it to age sixty-two before dying, and he seemed to be on the same path. Richard didn't let Marc or Georgina see it, but he jotted a quick note down: "Find a trainer." He understood the analogy. Their organization was the unhealthy patient.

"Then let's try to minimize the amount of time we use him by maximizing our rate of learning," he concluded.

"I don't want to look at the coach as the price for one person," Marc added. "I want to look at him as a subject matter expert that we are paying to have access to."

"Richard," Marc said, looking at him, "I don't want anybody worrying about the price for the coach. I don't want to see it as a line item and I don't want to discuss it. I will look at the overall cost we are investing and decide whether or not I think we are getting a good return. As soon as I feel comfortable, I will tell him that we no longer require his services. That could be three months or three years."

"Understood." Richard said.

"Thank you," Georgina said. "I promise that we will do our best, learning as much as we can, and producing the highest level of results."

"I'm confident you will," Marc replied.

That had gone about as well as she could've expected.

Looking back now, Georgina couldn't have imagined her team tackling this by themselves. There is no way they could've done it without a coach.

They assembled a great team, he made them read all of the best publications and encouraged them to go to seminars and conferences, and they still had a million questions. They simply didn't know what they were doing. They were enthusiastic, but they needed guidance. This was a critical juncture for them. If Marc hadn't supported it or prevented the ELT from scrutinizing it on a regular basis, they could've been sunk early. As CEO, he knew he had to be the champion.

Definition

The coach engaged early and regularly. He helped them craft their definition for innovation, without forcing his own on them. He did, however, think process was foundational.

Georgina had developed so much herself, as a person, as a leader and now as a healthcare innovation executive. Innovation. The term seemed so overused that it was almost without value during some of the conversations she had with colleagues from other systems. Along the journey, they had toyed with other terms and phrases but nothing seemed to capture the essence as well as this term did. They could've gone with a branded word, but building it and getting everyone to recognize what it actually meant would take more work than just explaining what her team meant by "innovation."

Process

There was a significant amount of debate around their definition and it probably took several months longer than it should have, but eventually they came up with their descriptive phrase: "Innovation is the output of a process that creates a disruptive product or service, simultaneously obsoleting the status quo."

It seemed simple, but there was a lot embedded in each word. The first was to get people to agree that there even was a process for innovation. She remembered Richard saying during one ELT meeting, "Can't you just get a bunch of smart people in a room and have something great come out?" His comment didn't seem that outlandish at the time, but looking back now, that would've been one of the worst possible things to do. Not because it was altogether bad—they certainly used that method during some brainstorming sessions—but because that did not create a systematic method that could be repeated. After reading the literature, attending conferences and seminars, but most importantly, talking to an expert, they settled on "process."

Disruptive

The next giant debate centered around the word "disruptive." The main problem was that when people brought up the word innovation, they all had a different idea of what innovation looked like. To one person, it was just something new. To another person, it was a fundamental technology shift that appeared to break the laws of physics. Popular authors discussed anywhere from three to six levels of innovation, each one having its own series of descriptions. One government agency even used a scale of 0-9 for technology! They had to settle on a definition that worked best for them. They wanted it to be aligned with the industry thought leaders as well. Some people wanted to include minor advances as innovation. There was one board member who took a solid stance only an industry-first technique could be considered innovation. How would they be able to find a common ground?!

Georgina reflected back on some of the discussions she'd had with her coach.

"Your innovation resources will always be finite, limited for numerous reasons. If you're going to have them work on something, you need to make sure they're at the sweet spot between effort and results," he said, likening the backlog of projects to rush-hour traffic on the interstate.

"Your organization already has a performance excellence team," he continued. "Their kaizen approach could handle simple levels of improvement and innovation."

She remembered how he would talk almost ad nauseam about the differences between PE and innovation. She couldn't think about that topic anymore; it would take too long. She'd have to flesh that out more when they formally started the documentation process.

Operational Lean vs. Lean Design Subsection

"There has been a lot of fuss regarding the similarities and differences between operational lean and lean design," the coach said, and sighed. The topic was exhausting to him. He hated operational lean being lumped in with lean design, yet it frequently was. It was no different here at Angstrom Health.

"Yes, there are similarities, like eliminating waste and maintaining flow," he began, "but they both have unique tools and unique applications."

"Respect for people and continuous improvement," Georgina quoted the two pillars of lean from memory.

"That's correct, we ascribe those as well. Let me explain the differences," he responded.

On a practical basis, continuous improvement usually was the dominant theme in lean work he had seen, and respect for people surfaced far less frequently, although much lip service was paid to it. There was no reason to bash operational lean. It was an excellent methodology, for operations. This was design, and their task was systemic innovation. A kaizen approach wasn't going to work here. They would not be setting up flow cells or conducting value stream analyses (VSA). Those were tools specifically created for daily, repetitive tasks with known demand. Their project had none of those attributes.

"The fundamental difference in operational lean is trying to eliminate variation, while lean design derives its entire value from variation."

"But what about the design process? Is that supposed to vary?" Georgina challenged the coach, having had years of exposure to operational lean.

"There will be a standardized design methodology. Every input will be unique and every output must be unique. The value is created by offering something new," the coach responded.

Lean loved standard work, establishing pull systems with kanban cards, having 5S work conditions, and one-piece flow. Zero defects was the mantra. Eliminate non-value-added steps. The coach knew some of the topics would cross-pollinate with lean design, but the techniques and skills needed to do the latter were so different that he hated to start with the similarities. When he had done so in the past, teams gravitated to all of the tools for operational lean and he had to pull them back one by one.

"That makes sense," Georgina said as she jotted that down.

"With your team, I am focusing on lean design, not operational lean. Therefore, I will start with the tools and techniques that are most important to our innovation work first."

He knew the PE team would have a strong opinion. They always did. He would address those issues on a case-by-case basis. For now, it was a lean design focus for innovation.

Product or Service

They did have quite a bit of work on the "product or service" part of the definition too. During her research, she found only a few dozen innovation centers associated with healthcare systems. She had reached out to most of them. The vast majority, almost all of them in fact, were focused on the product part of the definition. They were looking for ways to introduce new medical devices or software to the market. Many of them were birthed out of a desire for the doctors and surgeons to have a way to create something new if they really believed in it. Physicians don't know how to do product development. They certainly aren't ready for the hassles of getting Food and Drug Administration (FDA) approval. Commercial entities have their hands full with trying to do that part. Why would a hospital think they could be successful? There were a couple of examples where it had worked, but that was far from enough to convince the ELT. They all struggled, herself included, with understanding why a healthcare system would want to act like a start-up.

"We don't know how to manage technical risk. We don't have tens of millions of dollars to invest in a single piece of unproven technology. If we have a good idea, let's take it forward, but I'm not looking to be a medical device original equipment manufacturer [OEM]. We have enough issues taking care of patients. Let's focus on that part of healthcare delivery. That's our expertise," Marc stated during the earliest stages. She was happy they had come to a conclusion that would focus on changing patient care models, with the way they delivered medicine as the primary focus. That was how they came to the word "service." They could work or partner with medical device OEMs and tech firms if they stumbled onto a "product" idea.

Obsoleting the Status Quo

The last part of the innovation definition was "obsoleting the status quo." Here was where the levels of innovation played in a little bit. In order for the new product or service to be successful, it has to be able to replace the old one. It can't be something that goes alongside the existing solution. When patients use the new service, they should never want to go back to the old way. The power window switch on her automobile reminded Georgina of this. She remembered decades ago having to deal with a manual window crank to roll the windows up or down. That thing would make her arm sore going through all the toll booths. Toll booths were another thing of the past. She couldn't imagine going back to stopping, throwing change in a basket, and going. Those were both excellent examples of obsolescence. People like to bring up the smart phone versus flip phone, but that's a really big shift. It doesn't have to be that big to obsolete something. Her latest phone was evidence of that. It seems that screens keep getting bigger. She was over fifty, and this aided reading without her glasses.

The large text on the large screen was better, but this phone wasn't really different than her last one. Still, she wouldn't go back just one generation of smartphone. The new one was simply better for her.

She thought more about her phone. Her new phone was a nice, updated color, but innovation wasn't simply changing the colors. A kaizen team could do that.

"Yeah, I like the phone screen size example. I'll have to write that down," she thought out loud.

She did some mental gymnastics and figured it had probably taken a month or two before they had agreed to the definition of innovation. So many debates. Dozens of long discussions. Almost as many opinions as there were people. Anyone who showed any interest in her project had "words of wisdom." The irony was that her coach was the only one with real experience in the area. He must have explained it fifty different times. She would have to include a word of caution to new healthcare organizations trying to define innovation. Start with the definition they used, and modify it from there.

Beyond the Definition

Georgina remembered wincing when the coach told her what would be required to begin the formal effort, after battling just to define it.

"To begin with, you need dedicated space, dedicated resources and the framework," he'd said, acting like resources grew on trees.

"I might struggle getting all of those. I don't..." she started to say.

"These are table stakes,"

The coach switched to a health example. "Imagine you have a patient with multiple comorbidities. Let's say they have Type 2 diabetes, hypertension, and hyperlipidemia. They are obese and middle aged. You know if they continue their path, they are at risk of heart failure, amputations, or premature death. However, if they start now on proper diet and exercise, they can mitigate, maybe eliminate the risks."

Georgina flashed back to her conversation with Richard about paying for the Coach. Apparently he had gotten his own coach, as he was beginning to lose weight and talked about running a 5K.

"I see that all the time. We tell them they need to diet and exercise. They choose not to," Georgina shot back.

"Let me ask you this. For the ones it does work for, did they start with something simple?" Coach asked.

"Honestly, it's usually after an acute event or a poor prognosis that they get motivated."

"Your organization is at high risk for acquisition. Maybe not in the next couple of years, but there's nothing you're doing to differentiate yourselves. It is a stated goal of the board to remain independent. Your current health will not keep you there."

She had to agree. The analogy was perfect. It hit a little too close to home.

"Your patient has to start somewhere, right?"

"What?" She acted surprised. She had gotten so distracted thinking about her org that she had forgotten the patient scenario.

"You give your patient a starting point. You don't just dump everything on them at once."

Georgina chuckled to herself. A lot of her colleagues did just unload a ton of information on their patients. It must not have worked for them; otherwise the hallway conversations wouldn't have been filled with complaints about "non-compliant patients." She had abandoned that term long ago. She focused on finding a solution or two that would work for the patient.

"Point made," she admitted. "I present the facts, the alternatives, and what resources they have access to use. Often there is a little back and forth until we agree to a plan."

"Exactly. If they don't do the basics, they can't move forward. We have to have the basics too."

She knew this meant that a team, the space, and a formal framework were the starting point. It was tough being the patient. At least now she had a reference point to relate to her own patients. She could picture dietary changes and exercise routines. The framework would serve as the guide-book. She just had to figure out how to fund it and eventually what metrics to monitor.

Metrics

"If you're not measuring it, it's not important," the coach would repeat again and again. "We need a scoreboard for performance. Your patient scoreboard is their EMR. It gives lab values, values of vitals and other important measurements. You need metrics for your team," the coach told her.

"Which ones?" Georgina asked. The look she got back from her coach wasn't the one she was expecting. He didn't seem to like the question. "What's wrong?" she prodded.

"That is the million-dollar question," he deadpanned. "It's probably the question I get the most and it's probably the question with the biggest variety of answers."

"It depends" seemed like such a trite consulting thing to say, but it was definitely applicable here.

"Look, there are two basic types of metrics we can use. We can use ones to monitor our process and we can use ones to monitor our results. For instance, a diabetic can count carbohydrates, but ultimately they're trying to reduce their hemoglobin A1C. The first would be a 'driver metric' and the second would be a 'watch metric.' If you measure the first one right, then the second one should get where you want it. It's essential that we pick ones that modify the right behavior."

"Makes complete sense to me," Georgina replied.

"What are we trying to achieve right now?" the coach asked. "It will look different than what we are trying to achieve six months or a year from now. It will certainly be different from our steady state issues of the future."

"I will need to think about that a little bit, but I feel pressure to show progress to the ELT. They asked me for monthly updates."

"Not monthly," the coach almost interrupted. "Sure, you can formally report out to them monthly at their meeting, but you need to update the critical stakeholders much more frequently than that. I'm sure they don't like surprises, and it's never wise to expect an immediate decision when the players hadn't been prepared beforehand. You have to till the soil before planting."

As someone who enjoyed gardening on the weekends, she understood the reference. Each ELT member represented a different type of ground that needed to be prepared prior to formal meetings.

"So back to the metrics," the coach shifted gears.

They had taken a bit of a detour with that discussion. They were supposed to be talking about metrics and now he was giving advice on how to handle senior leaders. The coach would always allow some distractions. She just assumed that he felt the timing was right and the comment or question needed to be addressed. At first, it felt like her team wouldn't make any progress in meetings when he would allow a detailed discussion about a non-agenda topic. But he always knew to bring it back to the original issue they were discussing. Simultaneously, he was able to shed a little insight, giving them important knowledge about the why.

"We need metrics that will move the team forward and will cover issues the ELT will be asking about. You will need to decide on one or two that you're going to show them," he stated.

"One or two?" She could barely believe it. They're going to want five or ten, she thought.

"You're probably thinking they're going to want to see more," he said, cutting off her thinking, "but don't do it. They have enough numbers to worry about and we don't need to add a bunch more. If we can't show them with just a couple, then we're not measuring the right thing."

"So what do we start with? Number of ideas? Amount of targeted improvement?" Georgina offered.

"No. I want to start with what is important to us at the moment. For now, it's percentage of basics in place," he replied. "If we can't achieve those, we can't do what's next. Let's use team, location and meeting completion."

"That seems really basic, no pun intended," Georgina commented.

"You would think so, but I can't tell you how many organizations fail to assign people and give them somewhere to work," the coach said. "First, we will need to decide who should be on the team and then what we need to do our work. We're not going to ask for the world, but we are going to identify the minimal requirements."

"OK, let's define the team," Georgina said.

The Team

"I think of teams in three concentric circles, not unlike the cross-section of a tree," the coach started. "In the center we have the core team; next we have the extended team; and then, lastly, we have the ad hoc team, or curbsiders.

"The core team is made up of two or more individuals who are one-hundred-percent dedicated to the effort," the coach explained. "That may or may not seem like a lot of people, but I can assure you that without them being reassigned fully to this, the amount of effort needed will far outstrip the supply." The coach went on to explain that in organizations with large projects, this number could be in the hundreds. Healthcare, however, wanted as many people focused on day-to-day operations as possible and even one person being reassigned could seem like a lot. The coach preferred to have at least three to five people assigned full-time. In his experience, this was the critical mass needed to begin the cultural shift. It was his goal to gradually increase the team size to that standard.

"Why do they have to be one-hundred-percent?" asked Georgina. "Isn't it OK if they have another project or two they are working on?"

"If it was for one boss, I might consider it," the coach began to answer, "but it's almost always two bosses with two different agendas. As much as people want to cooperate and think they can work it out, it ends up a mess. I really can't compromise on this." The coach apologized for his tough stance on this one.

"OK, I will trust you. I will find two resources to immediately and completely assign to the team."

"Next is the extended team. These people spend twenty to fifty percent of their time on the team. This would include anyone with special subject matter expertise related to the project. This could be medical staff, nursing staff, providers or technical staff," the coach explained.

"A day a week?" Georgina was stunned. She wondered how she could find people who had enough schedule freedom to do that. It wouldn't be easy.

"This may not seem easy," the coach spoke for her. "But I guarantee if you find the right people, they will find the time."

There was more flexibility in healthcare than other industries. Many clinicians could decide what level of FTE they wanted to practice. Some could shift practice time over to administrative time. Others could be assigned a fraction of their time as administrative. Different health systems had different policies. Here at Angstrom Health, she would have to figure out how to make it work with their policies.

"The number of people will vary depending on the project," he said, as if reading her mind, "but I would expect this number to be somewhere around five."

"If they can't dedicate at least a day or week, then we can't use them." He made sure to drill the point home.

Georgina jotted some notes down.

"What about the last circle?" she asked, referring to the Ad Hoc portion of his drawing.

"That's actually the easiest one and the one most people are familiar with," he started to answer. "These are functional experts that we bring in as a consult on our solution. This could be an hour or two here or there or a half-day or full-day session. The main difference is they're not expected to participate every week. You just pull them in every now and then. However, we do like to formally name them so that both affected departments and the ELT know who we are counting on to deliver the project."

"I imagine this would include people like specialists, Information Systems (IS), or Human Resources (HR)," Georgina opined.

"You got it."

"All of this is project-based resourcing. What if we want to create a permanent team?" Georgina asked.

"Some modifications, obviously," he started. "Your core team would be bigger. Two isn't enough. Every project needs to have a designated leader. That leader can handle a maximum of two projects. If you're running multiple projects, you probably have enough work for your extended teams to be full-time. This would certainly include clinicians. You should have at least two clinical roles represented."

"That feels like the team is getting big." She paused briefly. "And expensive," although she didn't have to say that last part. The coach knew what she was thinking.

"If a board member suddenly wanted to set up a new service line because a relative had a rare disease or died unexpectedly from a certain condition, would she expect it to be staffed by two or three people?" he asked rhetorically.

"Now imagine asking them how many people they think they need to constantly obsolete their existing service lines on a regular basis to stay ahead of their competitors."

"They would never say hire two or three," she admitted.

"Marc is either committed or not. The amount of traction you get in an organization of this size is negligible with just a few people working on a project, maybe two at a time," he continued. "If we can't create five or ten openings, just stop now."

Angstrom Health was a two billion dollar system that operated two hospitals and dozens of specialty and internal medicine clinics. They weren't large, but they were no means small.

"It's almost enough to merit its own area but I think we should include it within the team," the coach added. "Every team needs a Project Chief, a single person responsible over it." There would be no dyads, a popular practice in healthcare combining a provider with an administrator as a two-headed leader. It was an answer for the egos and it didn't work in lean design.

"What qualities should they possess?" Georgina asked.

It was one of the most predictable questions the coach got when discussing this role. In reality, it took years, if not decades, to develop an ideal Project Chief, but most places didn't have the structure in place to do that and most certainly did not have the time to mentor one. He did his best to boil down the basics.

"First and foremost is project passion. They must become consumed with the patients' problems and creating a solution," he began. "This is frequently inversely proportional to tenure."

Georgina knew that was true. She had seen so many colleagues harden over their career, complaining about this or that and not wanting to adapt to new things. There were certainly exceptions. She would pull from that pool.

"Business and organizational prowess is next on the list," the coach said. "They need to know how it makes money for the business and they have to be able to drive the changes throughout the system. I don't except them to be financially savvy, but they need to understand the basics of how you make money."

That last comment helped alleviate some concern she began feeling in filling that role.

"I like them to have some level of technical depth. In healthcare, that usually means medical."

"Phew, an easy one," Georgina thought. "But maybe not a cheap one. She knew several providers that would like to try something new.

"The last area would be team players. There is too much work for a single person. It takes a lot of coordination."

Georgina knew there were lots of personality types and roles that had to be managed. Her pool of people shrunk again.

"Let's start with that," the coach concluded, as if it were easy, but it was just the start.

Patient Attrition Subsection

"I can guarantee you're losing a fair amount of your patient population every year. Now some may come back, but it isn't like old times. Brand loyalty plays second to provider relationship and convenience. Systems like to keep 'active patient' lists, but some of those lists are dated." He had run the numbers here and it appeared to be about 20%. Fortunately, they were regaining 15% each year in new patients. That still left a 5% net decrease. The coach didn't like to shed light on some brutal realities, but sometimes it took a major shock for his clients to pay attention.

Georgina had known plenty of patients who'd left when a fellow physician switched to a competitor. This also happened when the physician retired. A patient was more willing to switch at that point, since they had to "start from scratch." Their attrition was above average. Her coach was right.

She also knew a fair amount of patients who went to retail clinics, especially those with children who needed physicals for extracurricular activities.

He wrote the patient numbers on the whiteboard and they startled her. She wouldn't have guessed it was that bad.

"I also recommended someone from informatics and someone from your data department. They may not be full-time, but you'll probably use 0.6-0.8 of their FTE to start. Otherwise you become too burdensome on IS."

Georgina had experienced this before. The coach nailed that one. Joe didn't have patience for "our million random requests."

Metrics Subsection

"I'm sure the team set-up has something to do with one of the metrics you've picked," Georgina said, hopefully understanding what he was saying.

"Exactly! If we need people and they're not available, we want a record of that. It's a way for us to demonstrate that resources are needed to stay on track. If we get behind, this is one of the typical root causes. By formalizing it as a metric for the ELT, they can directly see our performance and help clear any barriers we might have," he explained.

That made sense to her. If there was anything that worked for doctors, it was the scoreboard for their performance. They were ultra-competitive and hated to lose. Identifying the team and reflecting the participation as a metric was an easy way to show if they were winning or losing.

The VP for Performance Excellence had pushed hard to have the innovation team as a part of his organization. The external coach had strongly disagreed and pushed back hard with the ELT. Things would have looked a whole lot different today if he hadn't.

"It simply doesn't work," he told the ELT, "you can't mix today's operations and the future. You will always sacrifice the future for the fires you're trying to put out today. When you do that, you will never build what the organization is supposed to be tomorrow. Operation and innovation need to have separate budgets, separate resources, and separate reporting structures."

He waited for any further comments or questions. There were none, so he moved on.

"Let's talk about the team, then."

Leader

Georgina was plucked from her role as a Specialty Chief. She had been a physician for over twenty years and still maintained a full panel of patients. Well respected as a physician, Georgina had a way of doing her job with excellence. Typical of a doctor, she had a great memory and was well versed on multiple topics. She stood above her peers with her no-nonsense way of getting things done. Her stoic demeanor betrayed reality.

Georgina loved to have fun and be a part of the crazy activities her team often participated in. In fact, many people were shocked to learn about her hobbies, families, and interests, given how hard she worked. She wasn't naturally outgoing but was quite comfortable with interpersonal conversations, no doubt bolstered by her years of interacting with patients.

This shift of roles surprised even her. She never imagined having such a high level of interest in something that felt far less scientific. It grabbed her attention and piqued her interest. Innovation became a web from which she could not extricate herself. She didn't want to get out of it. At this point in her career, she was facing big decisions on what was next. Chief Medical Officer was the expected route, but several were being considered. Other health systems, albeit smaller, had approached her for equivalent roles. She valued loyalty and commitment. It didn't make sense to jump ship from the only place she had worked.

It was Marc's initial request months ago that set the stage for where she was. He asked her to "fix" internal medicine. At the time, she had imagined a few things other places were doing. She had a laundry list of internal suggestions from herself and her team of providers.

The process of studying the entire delivery model opened her eyes to things she had never imagined. It wasn't doing internal medicine better that excited her. It was the process of being able to redefine healthcare. There was such a need for innovation in how care was delivered. Her team's research stoked the flame of enlightenment to a raging blaze. You couldn't know what she knew, have been exposed what she'd been exposed to and continue on a "normal" path. The transition to this new role became seminal for her future. If Angstrom Health didn't want to proceed, she would find another system. It was all driven by her passion to deliver better care for her patients and set an example for others. She was exactly where she wanted to be and needed to be.

Innovators

Innovators were Angstrom Health's equivalent of engineers. They did the most work and served on the core team. They started with two.

Ted Higgins was known as Hoggs. It came out of a quantum particle physics conversation they had. Was Higgs-Boson the God Particle, and what did that mean? Higgs was short for Higgins, but was too on the spot. They switched the consonants and got Hoggs-Bison. They started calling him that, but it was too long. He wanted to go by Bison, but it was easier to say Hoggs. Hoggs was a history major who'd made his way into healthcare nearly a decade ago. It would be tough to define him as either. He was organizationally gifted. He was very intuitive with people and had high emotional intelligence. He would eagerly apply his learnings and push the team to follow the process and achieve better performance.

Johnny went by the nickname Grand Luigi. At one point, he and another guy had created a wall-sized, eight-bit portrait of Luigi out of sticky notes. It was grand. Grand Luigi, they joked, about its creator. The nickname stuck. For practical purposes though, they called him Luigi. Luigi suffered from career ADD. He'd graduated with a degree in physics, taught ESL in Asia, done a stretch as a struggling musician, and then ended up in healthcare, courtesy of some good connections. He should have been a philosopher. He demanded deep, detailed discussion daily. Luigi asked all the tough questions others were afraid to ask. He required more detail than "just do it." He wanted to know the why. Like Hoggs, he was curious and loved learning. The two fed off of each other.

Physician

Suki was trained as a gerontologist. Outgoing and energetic, she loved helping humanity. She loved her Jewish father's heritage and her Asian mother's connection to eastern medicine. Taking care of patients with tough lives was her passion. She had only been practicing medicine for ten years but had made a name for herself at work. Suki had a broad worldview and readily welcomed new viewpoints. She was curious and learned at an incredible pace. Armed with a vast network, Suki had plenty of talented individuals she could reach out to on a variety of medical and non-medical topics. Highest-risk patients were the ones who impacted the system the most. If Suki couldn't help fix them, they wouldn't be able to address their most pressing issues.

PE – Ad Hoc

Theodore Kennedy was a know-it-all. There was already a Ted on the team, so they called him Kennedy. He was a Lean zealot, trained by the very Japanese sensei who created the methodology. To him, everything could fit under the Performance Excellence umbrella. After all, we were always looking to improve something, right? He had an answer for everything. To Kennedy, the entire world should be a mapped process, with all inputs, steps, outputs, information, materials clearly defined and monitored. He regularly used terms like flow cells, standard work, value streams, and waste. He constantly barked about accountability. There wasn't a metric he didn't like to track, display and discuss. Kennedy had actually made significant improvements to clinical operations. He was respected for the amount of savings his initiative had created, even if it had been painful at times. His team was quite large and deployed across the entire system. In fact, if you were an aspiring leader, you did an eighteen-month rotation in his group. Most, if not all, of the recently promoted executives had served in his department. Impact from the organization was felt everywhere. Templates abounded. People used a common vocabulary. Line level employees were directly connected to the strategic initiatives of the ELT. Most of operations ran as a well-oiled machine now. It wasn't that way at first. In fact, the first couple of years, it had looked like the whole thing might fail. It didn't. It had been around for years now and was embedded, quite possibly forever.

The success was a hindrance for the innovation team. Kennedy was a hurdle more than a help. He didn't directly attack innovation, he simply argued everything. He had one example after another of how "lean fixed it." He had been in healthcare for almost ten years now, but came from a career in manufacturing. Kennedy probably had another ten to fifteen years left in his career. He was comfortable. He wasn't going anywhere if he didn't have to.

He was initially brought in to help start the innovation effort with Georgina. It seemed like a really good match, but the two struggled to find a common solution. Kennedy just couldn't seem to get it through his head that Georgina was in charge. He had been interested in innovation for years and saw this as an opportunity to expand his personal experience. However, he was too entrenched in traditional PE methodology to make the jump to disruptive innovation.

The coach's focus was on Georgina and Kennedy was supposed to be an observer, perhaps documenting what he saw. Kennedy was too used to being in control. He didn't like Georgina's approach and was constantly taking the coach's time away from the team.

Finally, the coach approached the ELT and had Kennedy reassigned. There was some initial pushback, but Georgina supported it, hoping she could minimize the amount of energy she spent responding to Kennedy's passive-aggression. A lot of the team members wondered if they would face backlash on the decision with Kennedy still in the organization.

Honestly, it couldn't have been any worse with him off of the team than it was with him on it. Kennedy was a cancer that constantly worked against what Georgina and the coach were trying to accomplish.

Data - Core

Sheryl had access to the entire electronic data warehouse (EDW), a giant database of every electronic transaction of the hospital. Just knowing how to access the data was a graduate course in programming and configuration. She felt powerful but needed detailed requests. If one variable was missing or added, the entire data set could be wrong. Sheryl was used to working alone, in seclusion. It was just her and her computer. Her emotional intelligence level wasn't the highest and she often came across abrupt and unhelpful. She didn't play the best with others, often manipulating the data to tell her viewpoint. An eternal pessimist, she wasn't the best fit for an innovation team looking to shatter the current paradigm, but she was the only headcount that was available. Sometimes, Georgina wondered if her old department was trying to push Sheryl off onto her team.

Psychologist - Extended

Bruce Spluff held a PhD in psychology. He was a researcher with a firm grasp on what worked and what didn't. He joined the team after the first few months. He was relatively new to the organization, but that didn't stop him from fully contributing. He knew how underrepresented mental health was in healthcare. He himself had made a career change from Wall Street financier to psychologist following 9/11. He was eating in a first-floor restaurant at the World Trade Center when the first tower was struck by a plane. Large, falling debris had easily shattered the entire glass roof of the restaurant and proceeded to slam into the ground just yards away. Terror had filled him. He and the others sat hidden under a table for several minutes wondering what was next. Eventually he made it outside and began to help when he looked up and saw the second plane hit the exact floor where his dad's office was. Fortunately, his dad was late to work that day, having had an issue with his dog. The rest of his dad's company was killed that day. He knew them all. It was hardcore post-traumatic stress disorder (PTSD) that took him years to wrestle with and figure out how to handle. Bruce knew others had problems too. He worked with the Veterans Affair (VA) hospital during his doctoral research, helping military veterans get their lives back on track after seeing the horrors of war. He knew if there was going to be innovation in healthcare, then mental health had to play a central role. He was thrilled to be part of the team.

Nurse - Extended

Stacy was your above average nurse. She had all the traits of your typical BSN but more diagnostic capability. As with most nurses, she was most comfortable with a set protocol; however, that didn't stop her from thinking creatively. She had been a nurse for over a decade and was familiar with both inpatient and outpatient settings.

Stacy was passionate about delivering excellent patient care. It didn't matter if it was setting up intravenous medication, educating the patient about their condition, following provider's orders or comforting a family member, she loved all aspects of the nursing role. What bugged her was the lack of lower-level support for tasks that were in others' scope of practice who weren't RNs. Nurse Aids and Medical Assistants could and should have done more. This would have allowed her to focus more on what she was best trained and licensed for. She never complained about it, but she and her peers all felt the same way. This role seemed like an opportunity to begin to rectify that.

APC - Extended

They could have chosen a Physician's Assistant or a Nurse Practitioner for the role of Advanced Practice Clinician. Either would have worked well. However, given Valerie's push for expanded independence, they chose an NP. Georgina wasn't sure if they would get the person they wanted or not. To make things easier, she wanted to get someone who was already in a partial administrative role, and hoping to shift some of their practice time to additional administrative time for their projects. After chatting with both final candidates for the role, Georgina wanted Jose. He had begun to rise through the leadership ranks and was highly regarded with his experience. Her only fear was that he would consider this a career distraction. The other candidate was more readily available but not as passionate about pushing NP responsibilities to new levels. Georgina thought about meeting with Jose one more time but didn't want to seem desperate. He either wanted it or didn't. If someone had to be convinced to be on the team, they might become a liability. As much as she wanted Jose in the role, she didn't want the turnover risk from a partially committed team member. When the email showed up in her inbox, she was ready for either scenario.

Georgina,

Sorry for my delayed response. I had a family emergency to take care of and it took a couple days to catch up with my patients. I would be thrilled to be part of your team. It sounds exciting and I would love to represent the role of NP on it.

Jose

She was thrilled. That made it easy. Jose would bring a much-needed, forward-thinking perspective to complement the others on the team.

EMR Expert - Extended

After the consolidation of the electronic medical record (EMR) industry following the ACA-mandated implementation, there were only a few big players remaining. Unfortunately, EMRs became the thing that led, not clinicians. Everybody in healthcare were beholden to the EMR. In-house counsel used it as a defensive weapon against malpractice suits and CFOs used it as a glorified billing system. It became a significant burden for providers and their staff. Most healthcare systems had large teams strictly assigned to the maintenance and uptime of the EMR. OEMs were constantly updating the software and most were highly customizable on multiple levels. The IS teams rarely had time to respond to requests for improvements and would often put them in a nearly infinite queue. Because it was such a source of pain, it was mandatory to have an EMR expert on the team. That person would be able to tell them what could and couldn't be done. They could be proactive for future upgrades and maybe even help the vendors with functional improvements. Jake would serve well in this role.

"The team looks good," the coach stated. "Let's monitor how soon they are free and are regularly attending your team meetings once you set them up."

Georgina wouldn't include the extended team members during the reflection and documentation. They simply weren't around enough to place that workload on them. She would assign Suki, Hoggs, Luigi, Sheryl and herself as those responsible for fulfilling Marc's request.

Dedicated Space

"Your space should match your needs," the coach's recommendation still echoed in their head. "Maybe you start with an office or a conference room that you book full-time."

The team remembered because they wanted to do something amazing. In fact, they were using Apple and Google as their aspiration.

"You need to be you. Whatever environment allows you to do what you want, that's what you need," he had responded. "Don't try to be someone else, mimicking their space in hopes that you can be equally innovative. I can wear scrubs, a lab coat and a stethoscope, but that doesn't make me a doctor. Use it to inspire you, but become who you need to be."

Permanent Team Space

The team had never imagined that getting space for themselves would be so difficult. In the beginning, they were allowed to take over a conference room, but as the team grew, the conference room was no longer big enough. Besides, even if the team hadn't grown, the rest of the organization was growing impatient with not being able to use the conference room. It was silly, interoffice politics. They needed to find a new space. With the number of buildings owned or leased, this should've been a simple exercise. Even if there wasn't available space, they should be able to lease additional space if necessary.

She had scheduled a meeting with Jill and Sam, the director responsible for their facilities. He seemed eager to help them.

"What do you need?" Sam asked to start the meeting.

"We have a list of basics," Georgina began as she projected it on the screen. "We can talk about form factor. First, we need two project rooms. These will serve as the mission control centers for all of the projects. The room size needs to be at least sixteen by twenty feet. As much as we would like to have a higher amount of glass, we need as much wall space as we can. One of the walls should have a whiteboard across its width. We need to have an open space for desks and a conference room table and a small, private room in which to hold meetings. Ideally, we'd have an area to mark up and test our prototypes. The space doesn't have to be big but we would at least like it to be the size of a procedure room."

"Is that all?" Sam asked, somewhat sarcastically. Everybody was always asking him about available space. They had it, but the unofficial rule was taking it when it became unoccupied, and then, when they asked you about it, arguing that you couldn't give any up.

He wasn't expecting such a big ask from Georgina. He thought maybe a room or two in the same general area would suffice.

"I'll have to see what I can do and get back to you," Sam added. " I will talk to Jill to see whose department may have to give up some of their previous land grab. Also, we will have to talk to Richard about transferring the cost of the space to your budget."

"If we can't find it, we will look for a new location," Georgina responded.

"Well, I know they told you that in the meeting, but right now we don't want to increase the number of leases. In fact we are trying to consolidate some of our real estate," Sam told her bluntly.

"Also, I don't know what the budget is for renovation. I know they have been trying to keep that number low."

The look on Georgina's face must've told Sam everything.

"I'm sorry. Don't blame yourself. I'm just following their lead."

She had the budget. Now it was a bunch of bureaucratic red tape in her way. This type of stuff frustrated Georgina. She couldn't believe the amount of maneuvering that had to take place in order for her team to get their own official "office."

"This space can support a team size of at least fifteen people. If we grow beyond that, we will have to revisit the space."

"You need to plan on being in the space for at least three years," Sam said, sending another zinger into the conversation.

"Thank you Sam. I look forward to seeing what you can do."

With that, Georgina stood up, signaling the end of the meeting. It was a bit abrupt, but she was no longer in the mood for diplomacy. She had been looking forward to this meeting and it left a bitter taste in her mouth.

She had done her part and now it was up to Sam. If Sam failed to deliver, she would escalate to Jill and then to Marc.

Operating Mechanisms

"In order for your team to be effective, it requires two types of work," the coach's voice echoed in her head, "group work and independent work."

Reflecting back, she knew now that both were needed to ensure forward progress.

"Group sessions should accelerate the mass created by individuals. An acceleration that consequently will demand their effort afterwards," he said, alluding to Newton's second law of motion but emphasizing that it was a cycle of individual prep, team acceleration and individual follow-up that actually created great ideas.

Her coach wasn't particularly fond of the term "iterations." He felt that the word was an overused excuse for "rework," a lean term that denoted a fix for a defect. Defects were waste and so was rework. Iterations couldn't be used as an excuse to do a job halfway.

No, he preferred to use the example of a cyclotron, a device used to create radioactive isotopes, used in diagnostic imaging like Positron Emission Tomography (PET) machines to detect cancer and other physioanatomic anomalies in patients.

The cyclotron was essentially a particle accelerator, like those used by CERN to study quantum physics in an effort to understand the origins of matter. Instead of being kilometers in length, cyclotrons spin ion particles in a device that fits in a room. Strong, magnetic sources push the particles around and around until they reach the proper speed. Each revolution increases their momentum, over and over, until they approach the speed of light and are "shot" into an alloy target. This impact caused the particles to irradiate a basic medicinal solution, making it radioactive. The solution is immediately processed for intravenous injection.

Cyclotrons had to be close to the health systems using them. Immediately after creation, they began their radioactive decay, reducing the amount of usable isotopes. Some had mere minutes before becoming too weak to detect on the expensive equipment. Time was of the essence.

Yes, the analogy was strong. The team was the cyclotron. Their revolutions were the individual to group to individual work cycles. Their output had a limited half-life as well. The new services they developed needed to go to the market immediately, as they began to become obsolete the day they were introduced.

No, they didn't iterate; they accelerated. Their "particles" were the projects they worked on, broken down into sizes they could easily work on and launch. Agile called them "sprints," and a lot of clients were using the term already. He was fine using it, but he wanted to be clear that he didn't want their version of sprints to go on infinitely, with releases happening at the end of each until the end of time.

Governance

"I cannot stress how important the daily and weekly organization and tracking of activity is," the coach started. "Project governance is an area that requires organization and discipline."

Most of the team were creative thinkers and cringed at the thought of structure. It seemed so constricting. They were trying to break paradigms.

"I don't like the sound of this," Luigi said, stopping the flow of the discussion immediately.

"Just wait!" Hoggs took aim at Luigi. This was an area he appreciated. He had been on multiple projects over his career, and poorly run ones were a pet peeve of his.

"Let's try to keep an open mind. He hasn't steered us wrong yet. I don't think he's about to now," Georgina said, settling the troops.

"I'm not going to give you any more structure than necessary. You should know that this style of 'project management' can result in a fifty percent or more reduction in time. Said another way, if you don't do this, you can more than double the amount of time it takes to complete your project," the coach began again.

That was a significant factor. Any time you can cut something in half, people pay attention. This team was under significant pressure to achieve the fastest launches possible. As much as some of them didn't care for the highly structured portions, they knew they would have to in order to keep the ELT satisfied.

"There are three major areas that you need to have in place," the coach said as he picked up a dry erase marker and went to the whiteboard. He didn't like PowerPoints. It wasn't that he couldn't make them, he just found them not as engaging when teaching topics. People didn't pay attention or engage in dialogue as much when they had a printout in front of them or a projection of a slide behind him. No, he liked to create visual displays on the fly and he coached his clients to do the same.

- ■ Master Schedule
- ■ Team Meetings
- ■ Work Wall

"Are you sure the last one isn't the John Wall?" Hoggs asked as he did a little dance and sang, referencing a hip hop song about a basketball player from years prior.

The room laughed as the coach continued.

"The first thing that we need to remember is fluidity. Everything is dynamic. Things change all the time. There is no use in us planning everything to the nth level of detail only to replan everything a few days later. I never want to see a Gantt chart in this room and we aren't going to have the role of project manager."

Coach was referring to a classic, stage gate project management method he still ran into on a regular basis. Every time he stood in front of a project schedule, he would ask his client if it was accurate. Almost without fail the answer was "No, we just haven't printed out the latest version."

On top of that, he barely found others accessing it. He always felt that project managers used it as a tool to beat team members into submission to achieve an impossible deadline.

"As a team, you are going to create and maintain the schedule and required work yourselves."

Nobody in the room seemed terribly disappointed by this. Although they had minimal exposure to classic product development, several of them had been on IS or construction projects in the past and were looking forward to this new method.

"I can't wait to see this," Hoggs said, unable to hold back his enthusiasm.

"Surely you're not serious?" Luigi replied, not having the same level of excitement. He cut Hoggs off before he could finish.

"Please don't use the line from *Airplane*, Hoggs," Suki said, referring to the cult movie from her teenage years. "We know you're not Shirley."

Several of the team members groaned.

"I would never. That movie is so old. Luigi wasn't even born yet. Were you?" Hoggs asked.

He wasn't, but he had seen reruns on TV.

"The master schedule," the coach continued, despite the ADD moment of the team, "controls all important dates. It is a high-level calendar for project activities. Of highest importance are the release, or launch, dates. We do not want to change those."

"Launch something on time?" Hoggs chuckled. "I don't think we've ever been on time before."

It was true, but it didn't faze the coach. Virtually all the places he went struggled with keeping the original planned release date. One of the biggest issues was how that date was chosen. Random accuracy was the best way he could describe it. It went something like this—most executive teams were presented with a project and they would ask how soon the team could finish. The team would do some rough calculations and give a date that was way further than expected. The execs would balk and ask for it to be done sooner. Secretly or publicly, the CFO would ask about expected financial impact and then put that in the future projections. There would be a bit of frustration on both sides and a date would be chosen that didn't satisfy either party. Inevitably, the project would hit a bump in the road, from one of a host of reasons, and get behind schedule. One of the executives with the most at stake would push the team to maintain schedule. Trying to keep them happy, the team would try their hardest to stay on track but would usually fall behind more. The team leader would start to ask for schedule relief, a little at first and then more later. Execs would balk once again, and the team would "see what they could do." Eventually, the executive team would accept the fact that the project would not be done on time. The schedule would slip. It could be weeks, months or even years behind.

"Being on time starts with strategically choosing the release day," the coach responded.

"That's easy to say, but what does that mean?" Georgina asked.

"When we pick a date, it's going to be for an important reason, not 'ASAP,'" the coach stated. "It will correlate with another cycle. For instance, it could be a new way to administer flu vaccines. We would clearly need to be ready by the beginning of flu season. Maybe it's fall physicals for school sports, or it could be to present findings at a trade show like GPIN or AMGA."

Their faces showed that it seemed to make sense to the team. They likely didn't know enough either way, the coach thought. That could be an advantage over those with cultures of tardy launches.

"We will use our release date as a constraint. When we are doing feasibility on our solutions, only those that meet the time criteria will advance, others will have to be rejected or postponed to the next release," the coach explained.

Blank looks meant he needed to explain a bit more.

"Let's say we find a great module to add to our EMR but IS can't get to it until the following quarter or the next year. We're taking that solution off the list. We'll have to find another option to work instead."

"But what if that solution makes or breaks the project?" Suki asked.

"Then we have a big decision to make. By strategically choosing our release date, we are committing to an entire series of activities from multiple functions. When we change it, it throws everyone off. Some team members may no longer be available, budget could shift to other needs, or any number of problems. If it truly is make or break, we will have to present to the ELT and they will have to decide which tradeoff to make."

They hadn't thought about the chain of events. Of course, it made sense; it just seemed much easier to say than do.

"For your team to be ultimately successful, release delays must be the exception, not the rule. Our motto will be 'on time, every time.'"

"OK, so we put a lot of thought into the release date. What else goes on there, especially if it's not going to look like a Gantt chart?" Hoggs asked.

"The master schedule is going to be split in thirds, with the length of each portion determined by the functions most required during each."

"Thirds? Is this stage gate?" Sheryl asked incredulously. She was a major proponent for an Agile approach and was used to working in short iterations.

The coach had pushed the team hard all morning. It was time for a break. Not a fifteen-minute one. A long one. They could include lunch as well.

"We're taking a field trip," the coach stated.

Spontaneity and innovation go hand in hand. Not everything is structured. There are times for it and times it hinders. Right now, the coach knew everyone's brain was hurting and they needed an outlet.

"Where to?" Luigi asked.

"Somewhere inspirational," the coach responded.

"We'll grab lunch from a food truck and eat it on location."

The team loved food trucks nearby. The food quality was good and the variety was excellent. The inspirational part confused them. Their existing culture always ate at their desk or a quick bite in a restaurant. "Inspirational" was never on the menu.

"I found a trail through the woods that goes to a river," he told them, wondering how they would respond.

"It's not far, is it?"

"Do we have time?"

There were a couple of sceptics, but none that weren't pressured into going by the enthusiasm of the others.

"Hey, he's teaching us and you're getting in the way,"

"Seriously, just go with the flow."

"Alright, let's do this!"

The field trip took two hours. They went to a nearby state park no one on the team even knew existed. The coach had checked it out the evening before. He didn't rush the team, but he didn't waste time either.

When everyone reassembled in the room, the energy was high. People were laughing, sharing photos they had taken and getting along well. The coach would take them on more trips and force them into more spontaneous activities. It helped build the culture in ways conference room training could not.

Agile and Stage Gate

It was now time to address the stage gate comment Sheryl brought up prior to the field trip. Agile had become ubiquitous in software development and was making significant headway into a variety of industries. Almost every IS department claimed to use an Agile approach. The reality was much different. It was rare that the coach came across an organization that truly practiced Agile principles. There were a few common disciplines he saw regularly pulled from Agile. True practitioners would cringe at what some organizations were calling Agile. Sheryl clearly believed in Agile, at least her version of it. She had been certified as a Scaled Agile Framework (SAFe) coach and let everyone know it. The coach chuckled at the thought. Anyone with a week of time and a minimal budget could get certified. Most never brought an Agile coach in to see how they were doing. It frequently resulted in their own organization's flavor of Agile, often far from the original recipe.

In addition, Agile had limitations for non-continuous release applications. He knew that any time the changeover costs in "retooling the organization" were high, constant releases were worse, not better. This was something he and diehard Agile coaches agreed to disagree on. The coach hadn't seen any Agile transformation that figured that problem out.

Ultimately, the biggest difference between stage gate and Agile was the size of the batch created. Agile, a Lean-based methodology, pushed for constant flow, focusing on small, iterative releases, one after the other, in perpetuity. Stage gate tended to batch groups of releases together into bigger releases. Website changes were the ultimate expression of Agile and massive projects like canals or aircraft carriers, were the quintessential waterfall projects. There would always be batches. Their size, quantity, timing and how they were managed would vary. Agile was very prescriptive in each of those areas. It allowed practitioners to follow a strict protocol. The coach found some useful and others not. Ultimately, a business existed, even healthcare, for its customers. If you had no customers, you had no business. Growth occurred when people thought your product or service was a better value than everyone else. They voted with their spending. Profit meant some future life expectancy. It was up to the business to manage costs to be profitable. Here, patients were the most important piece of the puzzle. If Angstrom Health maintained or grew that number while controlling costs, their future was safe. There were elements of Agile that enabled that and others that placed speed ahead of that. The coach would ensure the team here had the best of both worlds, custom tailored for their innovation maturity.

"We will use some techniques that are similar to Agile. We will not attempt to be Agile," the coach flatly stated.

Sheryl seemed offended by his position.

"We will also use some techniques that appear to be stage-gate-based," he added.

"Our master schedule will feel like a waterfall approach. Now, each section of the schedule can vary in length. "We might be able to run some things through all three stages in five minutes or less. We do that every time we pick a place for the team to eat lunch. Realistically, we should aim for a minimum of one month and a maximum of three months for each stage," the coach recommended.

The coach understood Agile, Scrum and Sprint, but he didn't like all of the elements. He really liked part of the scrum portion of Agile, in particular how the sprints were organized and run, so he used a modified approach for his clients. Angstrom Health had done well in adopting it.

Team Meetings

"I have six rules for team meetings," the coach said as he approached the white board and wrote them down.

1. In person.
2. Every week.
3. Take notes.
4. Discuss delays.
5. Make decisions.
6. Plan the future.

"What if we're not onsite for the meeting?" Suki immediately asked, knowing several of them had clinic days at another location.

"I do not want to see a dial-in number in the meeting invite. Be there in person unless you're on vacation or a business trip. There is no reason to miss this meeting. Together you will decide what day of the week and what time works best. For the first several weeks you may have a couple of conflicts you need to deal with. In the future, do not double book over this time, for anything," he sternly stated.

"You're pretty serious about this," Hoggs observed.

"Conference calls are a last resort. There are so many things wrong with them I won't even begin to explain them all. Be at the meetings, in person, period. Nothing is as effective as face-to-face [F2F]." He was very clear. He had experimented with all types of virtual solutions. It didn't matter how realistic it was, it didn't achieve F2F results yet. Maybe someday virtual reality (VR) or augmented reality (AR) would achieve it. Until then, there was no reason for a team based in one location to dial in. They would have to be disciplines in their schedule management.

"Why weekly? Why not daily or bi-weekly?" Luigi asked.

"Excellent question. Several reasons," the coach answered. "The work doesn't change enough each day to pull the entire team together. When you're going every other week, people are always wondering if it's this week or next and attendance falters. It's easy to know you need to be somewhere every Thursday at 10 a.m."

He didn't care what day or time, just that the team had determined one.

"Schedule it for an hour. If you get done before that, end the meeting. If you're consistently going over that, you'll need to revisit how much you're trying to get done. It shouldn't take more than an hour," he finished.

"We chose weekly and it worked for us. The coach was right," Georgina reflected.

"As far as meeting notes, we follow the protocol we discussed earlier," Hoggs noted, moving on to the next topic. "We tried a few different ways to distribute the notes and settled on software that accepts a combination of handwritten notes, photos and typed text. We store it in the cloud by title and date."

"The last three items are the standard agenda for every team meeting," the coach said.

"We always made an agenda and emailed it out every week," Georgina admitted. "And he asked us 'Why? That's too much work.' We pushed back at first, but he wouldn't let up. It took a few times, but then we realized it really was a waste of time."

"The worst thing about meetings is that they can turn into talk fests for a couple of people, while it's a snooze fest for everyone else," the coach explained. "Meetings should be tight. Once everyone is there, on time, you can focus on it being a working meeting."

"We always start by discussing any delays we're facing. Do we need help? Does it require a countermeasure to fix?" Georgina said. "People don't like to be late but we always discuss ways to get back on track. We don't like to leave people hanging and the coach doesn't like us to change the due date, like ever."

"It sets a bad standard, just changing dates. If something is being actively worked, it needs to be finished when the team needs it. You need a way to escalate up the management chain based on days late if you constantly struggle to keep dates," the coach recommended. "People don't like their boss's boss finding out they're behind. It makes everyone look bad, and you know what rolls down hill.

"Don't hold a meeting if you aren't going to make a decision. Projects don't have time for pontification and bloviating." This was clearly a touchy point for the coach. "Meetings single-handedly ruin productivity when decisions aren't being made."

"For each item we are working on, we like to share our findings, make a recommendation and then decide. We might debate it but we make a decision and we record it. It makes the whole thing very tidy. Everyone is engaged," Suki explained.

"For any given meeting we make half a dozen or more decisions. Some weeks we can make ten to fifteen of them," Hoggs added. "It's a very effective focus. Most of our meeting is spent on making these decisions."

"Lastly, we look at what work is coming up and plan for it. We ask a bunch of questions," Luigi noted. "Are we doing enough? Is the work well distributed. Do we need to shift anything around? What new things should we be considering or looking into? Inevitably, some of our decisions create more questions."

"And that's good," Hoggs interrupted. "Because it's usually the right timing and it makes our project stronger."

"We like to watch the master schedule and see if we're on track. The worst is to be caught off guard by something big and have to rush work just to get it done. It's sloppy and everyone can tell," Suki said.

"The type of work we do shifts based on what stage. We're answering questions in the Research Phase, Developing and Testing in the Exploration Phase and doing task completion in the Delivery Phase." (Stages discussed in Chapter 3.)

"Some of us like some stages more than others. I would be happy just to do the Research Phase all the time, because I'm a dreamer. The Delivery Phase annoys me. It feels really checklist-y," Luigi admitted.

"But we need to maintain continuity and our team is very small," Georgina replied. "So every core team member is on for the duration of the project."

Work Wall

Georgina remembered the conversation that day about the work wall. It seemed like eons ago.

"You need to visualize what work needs to be done. At the top of the work wall should be the master schedule. It drives the overall project. Include the critical releases and each of the RED stages," the coach began.

Sheryl wasn't satisfied, but the coach didn't care. He had seen too many examples of Agile gone wrong. The arrogance of the software world thinking Agile works equally well everywhere was too much. He wasn't going to let Angstrom Health go down that path. They needed discipline and process first. Maybe someday, but not anytime soon.

"The focus of this wall should be what needs to be done in the next month or two. Anything beyond that should be outlined at a high level on the master schedule," the coach emphasized. "No details." He drove the point home.

"Project effort will have three main buckets of work: the incoming queue, what you're working on and what decisions have been made. I don't care what you call each of them. It could be Backlog, WIP, Completed, like in Agile, or it could be Next, Now, Done. Pick something and use it. For now, I will call them Queue, Ongoing and Decisions."

"Each piece of work that needs to be completed should have its own card."

"What do you mean by card?"

"It could be a literal note card, a sticky note, or eventually an electronic 'card' once the process has been locked in," he answered. "But I like to see everything in physical form for at least the first project."

"We wanted to go direct to electronic but when we tried it was clunky, even with the variety of software and apps out there," Georgina noted. "We went back to sticky notes. They just work really well."

"Color coding the cards for feature or need correlation is very helpful. Agile likes to put the User Story on the back of each, but it's impractical to write on the back and then use it," the coach told them.

"Content for the queue should be created as a combination of formal sessions and impromptu reasons. Anything can be added at any time," he continued. "Each card needs to have a single action on it, no more.

"All of your project effort has a shelf life, an expiration date, if you will," the coach explained. "If something has been up there for several weeks and nothing has been done to complete it, you need to ask if it's critical or not. If it is, it needs to be completed immediately. If not, take it off the wall. It's a distraction."

"At first, we were extremely uncomfortable taking things off the wall without completing them," Luigi recalled. "We spend so much time coming up with what needs to be done and want our result to be the best. Sometimes our hopes were too high and we wrote things down that would be nice to have. It's tough to complete everything. When so much time goes by, we have to acknowledge that and address the elephant in the room: We aren't able to get this card done."

"It's painful because it almost always results in some tradeoffs that impact our final solution," Suki added.

"At one point we got really behind on a project and wanted to clear a bunch of cards by eliminating them. It was early in the project and required a lot of researching. It would have been easy to get rid of them, claiming they were too old. In fact, it would have meant we effectively skipped a stage. Our coach pushed us to complete them. It was a good thing we did. We learned stuff from those cards that had a major positive impact on our project. Be rigorous about removing cards from the wall," Luigi concluded.

"Best practices around each card include standard formatting, even if it is handwritten," the coach had explained. "In addition to what you're doing and the color coding, you will need a spot for a Harvey Ball* to track completion, the person responsible for the card, and a target completion date."

For the Harvey Ball, we only use quadrants with the following definitions," Hoggs said as he wrote on the whiteboard.

 0% - No work done
 25% - Direction discussed and work assigned
 50% - Ongoing work taking place
 75% - Good progress being made
 100% - Completed with decision

---

* A Harvey Ball is a circle divided into four "pie" quadrants.

"People get some freedom in choosing what to work on. They manage their personal workload, pulling work from the queue when they have capacity to work on it. We like to have a date by the end of the active sprint," Hoggs explained. "We don't put someone's name on it until it has been pulled by a team member as active work. Once it leaves the queue, it should have a Harvey Ball, a name, and a completion date."

"As we work it, we update the Harvey Ball. When the work is complete, we present the findings and make a decision about it. When the decision is made, we add it to the card or over the card and move it to Completed," Luigi chimed in.

"We accumulate our Completed Cards until a release is complete. It adds up, but the history is always right in front of us," Suki added.

Sprints

"Eventually, if you find other elements of Agile that you like, by all means experiment with them and adopt the portions that work for you. However, I want you to focus on a modified Sprint as your starting point." The coach's words echoed in their memory as they reflected back to the beginning.

"Just think of a sprint as a period of time when you're committing to a set amount of work," the coach explained.

"Agile likes to do a whole work breakdown structure for each card in a Sprint, determining the total amount of work and monitoring it using a series of charts."

"We were so eager to be Agile that we wanted to do those too," Luigi noted. "It was way more cumbersome than it was useful. With a small team, it was overkill."

"We didn't like the feeling of due dates," Luigi commented. "It was uncomfortable having accountability."

"It didn't feel enabling." Hoggs paused. "At first."

"We love sprints now. We experimented with sprints a week to a month in length but settled on one-month sprints," Suki said. "It gives us enough time ahead and work to do without being overwhelming or too slow. Eventually, I think we'd like to go shorter but it's working for now. We like to have something working at the end of each sprint, not just another block of time completed."

"We have to stick to our decisions. Once cards are complete and a decision is made, we don't like to revisit them. We consider them closed unless absolutely necessary," Georgina stated. "Otherwise, it can be like unraveling a thread, impacting several other areas that were already done too."

Chapter 3

Basic Tools

Flashback

"The basics? Ha! It would probably be the equivalent of telling an over-weight patient that they had to run a mile. It wouldn't be a big deal for a marathoner, but if someone sat on the couch all the time and was one hundred pounds overweight, it would be a whole different story. It was the same with getting this innovation center up and running. Getting the basics set up was necessary," Georgina thought, remembering when they had started, "but it took time and a lot of effort."

She related it to one of her patients. He had gotten overweight as an adult and eventually became diabetic. Exercise was no longer a part of his routine and his food choices were bad. For some reason, a light bulb went off in the patient's mind following one lab test. She watched his transformation after that conversation. He had a follow-up appointment a few months after she shared his lab results. He had already lost a fair amount of weight and was riding his bike several miles at a time. Although his diet wasn't perfect, he was eating much better. The patient was extremely optimistic about his health once again and was happy with the direction he was headed. He still had a lot of work to do, but he was on the right path.

"That was us, too," she thought, likening her innovation team to the patient. "We had to start with the fundamentals. We had no idea what we were doing. Those first few months, we learned a lot and got on track."

Not all of the executive team were patient. A couple, including the CFO, were constantly pushing her to show results way faster than the team was delivering. Georgina would use her patient example with the executive team, reminding them that from an innovation perspective, they were as overweight and out-of-shape as they come. She made a list of the basic tools they had to learn and apply appropriately.

1. Team Communication
2. Meeting Notes
3. Patient Focus
4. Pugh Matrix (Test Clinic)
5. Queue
6. Analytical Hierarchy Process (AHP)
7. Failure Modes and Effects Analysis (FMEA)

Team Communication

The team needed a way to communicate amongst themselves. Email alone would not cut it.

Their IS department did not like this and kept telling them to use email for everything. In the beginning, they did what they did for any project regarding IS: they ignored their opinion, experimented and then formalized. IS was always so slow to get on board. They were always busy with keeping up operations; they never had time for them. In fact, it wasn't until they got someone to join in as part of the team meetings that they began to make any progress. The problem wasn't at the leadership level; the CIO supported their efforts. However, he couldn't sit around and approve every request that came through. He had a division to run. When the team needed help, they had to go down the ranks to find someone with that specialty. That was where the problems happened.

Eventually, they would settle on solutions for three different areas:

1. Official communication
2. Instant communication
3. Social communication

Official communication was always routed via the Angstrom Health email server. It was available on their computers as well as their mobile devices, so it worked fine. Since their inbox would back up with corporate emails, other system reminders and a variety of time-draining messages, the team did not rely on email for speed.

If there was something a team member needed quickly from someone else, the default choice would be a quick face-to-face. Although the team was co-located in a single facility, Georgina preferred that her team talk to each other. If someone was in the next room, you didn't send a text or an email. You walked into the room, made sure they weren't busy, and shared the information. Although society had grown fond of electronic communication, and emoji use helped with the tone, it was too easy to misunderstand the sender's statement or question.

If the person wasn't available face-to-face and the information or response was short, the team used text messaging between their mobile devices. Georgina didn't believe in a long exchange of lengthy texts. If the expected response was more than a phrase long, the team members were required to call each other. There was some loss of asynchronicity but overall the team found they worked better and faster that way.

Finally, the team wanted a way to be social without posting their stuff for the public. They experimented with a few apps and settled on one that would allow them to maintain privacy but exchange funny comments, team photos or other entertaining messages. Something was posted nearly every day. It was a way that the team could bond and access group experiences without outside eyes. Indeed, if other departments had seen their feed, at times they would wonder if the team ever got work done. Ironically, this was one of the things that enabled the team to be the most productive one in the entire health system.

Of course, all communication that contained personal health information (PHI) required a HIPAA-compliant protocol—one established by their IS department and followed by all.

Meeting Notes

"Why don't we talk about one of Luigi's favorite topics, meeting minutes?" Hoggs joked, knowing that Luigi had struggled with them at the beginning. The team no longer made their own personal records during meetings; they took inconspicuous team minutes. Everyone could see the notes and had a chance to read the verbiage. If it needed an adjustment, someone would just chime in. They had to be singing from the same sheet of music. In the past, small variations of what one person recorded versus what was intended had added weeks to the project. Now, every-one got a single version. People still took some personalized notes for themselves, but they didn't record the meeting. It allowed everyone to focus on the meeting and its content, not on documenting ten versions of the same thing. This was quite different than this organization had ever seen before. In fact, in healthcare, people are trained to take their own notes.

"Standardize repeatable processes," their coach would say. "You want to focus your creative energy on the non-repeatable parts of the job. Trust me on this."

Trust me on this. How many times had the team heard their coach use this line? It drove them crazy. We can't "just trust you on this," they would think to themselves. You have to "prove it to us." Finally, one of them told the coach he had to prove it instead of their simply "trusting him."

"OK," he said, "we're going to take meeting minutes this way for three months. At the end of three months, if you don't think it's the best thing ever, then we'll go back to how you're doing it now."

For people who like to dream and innovate, this was a hard concept to grasp. Standardization was the enemy. Any time there was a stan-dard, it felt like putting on a straight jacket. It felt very uncomfortable and constricting. Both Hoggs and Georgina appreciated a standard when one existed, but Luigi bristled at them. Even so, having one set of meet-ing notes took quite some time before it was fully adopted. When it was, they looked like this.

- Title of the meeting at the top center of the page.
- Page number on the top right of the page.
- To the left of the page number, the date.
- Below the page number, the list of attendees at the meeting.

MEETING MINUTES

NAME OF THE MEETING	2/14/2018	✓
SUMMARY POINT IS LISTED HERE. COULD BE A DECISION OR A FOLLOW-UP		ATTENDEE
NEXT SUMMARY POINT GOES HERE. SHOULD INCLUDE A NAME AND DATE IF NEEDED.		ATTENDEE
THE LANGUAGE OF EACH SUMMARY POINT SHOULD BE AGREED BY ATTENDEES.		ATTENDEE

There were only three things included in the meeting minutes:

1. Decisions made during the meeting
2. Upcoming important dates
3. Items that needed follow-up

Of course, for all the items that needed follow-up, they had someone's name and a due date attached.

They didn't use Robert's Rules of Order. There was no creating motions or seconding. It wasn't some big formal to-do. They simply took the notes publicly using the base standard format. The team still pushed back.

To make matters worse, their coach forced them to write the meeting minutes on a whiteboard or a flip chart. This seemed so old-fashioned.

"Why don't we just type them in?" Luigi argued.

The coach took on the accent of a Japanese martial arts sensei, not unlike Miyagi from *Karate Kid*.

"Grasshoppa, technology not solution by itself. Technology only good answer if for actual problem. Plus, must learn process first. Wax on. Wax off," the coach countered, actually repeating a line from the well-known movie.

Luigi didn't like it, but he got the point. The coach wanted them to learn a paper process before choosing a digital solution. He remembered making that statement and getting kudos from the coach. Actually, now, Luigi was one of the most responsible for using this technique. He had become an evangelist and a disciplined practitioner of it.

Georgina remembered pushing back at the beginning too, but for different reasons. Now, she had fully adopted it, although at times she found herself still slipping back to her notebook in small meetings, courtesy of decades of practicing medicine.

"It also works as a method to build consensus. We're sticking in a one-line summary of a conversation that may have been fifteen minutes. We want to make sure that the summary captures the essence of the conversation from everyone's perspective. Before meeting minutes, there was always a messy interpretation of some point. Since then, everyone on the team has gotten familiar with saying, 'What did the meeting minutes say?' It stops the argument every time. Frequently, we have had to rewrite a point to make sure that everyone was OK with it, whereas before everyone had their own version," Georgina stated.

"We thought we would immediately switch over to a digital format," Hoggs interjected. "I mean, I was ready to do that on week two. We ran a couple of small experiments but found that we needed to project things on the screen while simultaneously taking notes. It wasn't until we added a secondary screen that we were able to make the switch to digital."

"Don't forget about your template," Georgina said.

"Oh yeah, we didn't want the digital version to vary from one person to the other. I created a template that was accessible on the cloud. It was easy to input and display the meeting title, date and attendees in a consistent way. Now when we view them, either online or printed, they all look the same. They're all stored on the cloud as well. We have a standard naming format so it's easy for us to find what we're looking for," Hoggs added.

"It actually took a couple of meetings to agree on the file nomenclature," Georgina said, "but we can find those actual meeting minutes and show anyone the original document from when we decided."

Patient Focus

The coach was relentless about understanding the customer. His voice echoed in their ears: "The biggest waste in creating something new is making something that nobody wants."

He wanted to see how well they knew this topic, so he told them to act like they were sitting on a panel at a conference explaining this to an audience. Sheryl was out of the office that day, so he set up the front of the room with four chairs and took the position of the audience.

"OK, let's see what you know," he told them.

They had each prepared note cards to read from, but they hadn't rehearsed like they would have for a conference. All of them took a seat at the front, looked back and forth at each other, and then started.

Deep Customer Understanding

"It may sound simple, but it's not easy to do. What do you do when you formalize what patients want? You get a bunch of people in the room with a whiteboard and within thirty minutes, you have a list of their needs. But you're wrong. We were wrong. You have to assume you don't know," Suki started off.

Pretty bold introduction, the coach thought, telling healthcare they're wrong. But he didn't object.

"Especially as a physician," Georgina added. "I always feel like I am right and I'm training the patients. At the beginning of my career, I wouldn't even listen to what they had to say. When they were talking, they sounded like Charlie Brown's teacher, 'Wah Wah Wah.' I wasn't even listening. When they got done, I would just tell them what I was going to tell them before they started talking. I think it's pretty easy for us in healthcare to assume we know what the patient wants. By going through this process, we realized how silly that was."

"During one experiment we were running," Luigi interrupted, "the team was asking her patients specific questions related to a project. One of those patients she had been seeing for nearly twenty years. She didn't even realize that the patient preferred to go by a nickname until we discovered it.

"I was embarrassed," Georgina said. "It really forced me to start listening more and stop making assumptions."

"After all," Luigi added, "they are the experts in getting our services. They know what they want better than anyone. We only know what works best for us."

They went ad-lib there, he noticed. That was fine; they should probably include that anyway.

Getting Ready

"There are a few things that you need to know before going into the data collection itself," Suki started again. "Ask open-ended questions. By far the worst question to ask the patient would be a yes or no question, especially related to whether or not they would like or use a new service. There are two reasons for this. While some will say no, most people won't want to make you feel bad. It's easy to take that information and say that the majority of people say yes. The other reason is that you get no context. Sure, you could ask why afterwards, but the responses are never as rich."

"We found we have to focus on listening, not talking," Luigi began. "We have to talk enough to get the people to feel comfortable, and then let them speak. You're interviewing them, not vice versa. As the interviewer, you want to be the one who is absorbing information from them, the expert. You can't do that if you're talking. Your questions should be natural based on what their response is. You don't want to suddenly change topics when they're in the middle of something very important to them. If you're thinking about what you want to say, you miss this. Remember to listen and listen well."

"Also, we capture every word of a conversation," Hoggs added. "I guarantee people are going to want to push back on this one. We sure did. The problem is, if you don't, you introduce a significant amount of bias with your version of the notes, even subtle things such as word choice or context. You may think that you'll never forget that comment or suggestion, but after your seventh interview, it all starts to blur together. Even a week later you'll have forgotten more than you expected. Capturing every word of a conversation allows you to go back to verbatim comments and pull them out. They are the most powerful. It also allows you to revisit parts of the conversation that you have forgotten or highlight ones that people need to hear."

"There are several ways to capture every word," Luigi said, continuing Hogg's thought. "But we recommend creating a recording as a backup. With smartphones, this is super easy. We like to error on the side of caution, so we have every patient sign a recording permission form. We assure them that it will never be used outside of the project team. Given that most patients are comfortable with the privacy of healthcare, they're usually very trusting on this. We work hard not to violate that trust. In addition to the recording, we will either perform a live transcription or send the recordings away to be transcribed. However, it took us a while to get approval for the transcription services, and we created many of the early ones ourselves. We are looking forward to the day when speech-to-text capability can handle lengthy conversations, but until then, we will transcribe the recordings.

"Get through the superficiality," Hoggs said. "First they may want to compliment you and not be critical. They will tell you how much they love about this or how much they like so-and-so. The conversation has to go beyond that. Even the nicest, happiest people will have some things they don't love about the service you're currently providing for them."

"Suspend judgment," Suki said. As a doctor, this was hard for her to do. "It will be easy for you to start to hear a recurring theme and to focus on that. You have to assume that there are more things that bother them or more things that you can do to fix it. Be careful not to get stuck in a rut."

"Look past solution ideas," Georgina cautioned. "Patients have a tendency to give you specific ways to fix things. While those may be good, you need to ask yourself why that idea seems attractive to them. In fact, you can ask them, what is it about that idea that you like? They're more than happy to tell you."

"Prepare questions, but be ready for the conversation to go off script," Luigi noted. "We always have a list of questions that we want answered during a patient interview. Rarely do we get through one hundred percent of them. However, the tradeoff is always for richness of content. This one builds off of listening well. It requires you to not just pay attention but to probe into different areas that they bring up. Some things may throw you completely off-guard. If you're just looking at your script and what questions you have to answer, you'll miss a golden opportunity. Be prepared to talk about side topics in order to understand context."

"Hardcore researchers and statisticians don't consider the number of people we use for our interviews as 'statistically significant.' That's OK." Hoggs added. The coach had emphasized this over and over.

"If you follow Angstrom Health's lead, then you will be light-years ahead of what most people do," the coach thought to himself.

"We have found that we can use a follow-up survey that will give us research-quality results if we eventually want to publish the results," Suki added. "We have to keep in mind that what we are doing is far from the norm. We like telling patients what to do, not the other way around. Listening to even a few dozen can have dramatic impact on anyone hearing it."

"Here are the main collection points and what we do," Hoggs said as he went to the whiteboard and began writing. They would likely have to do this in presentation software at a conference, but that would be overkill for this mock run.

Directional Check

QUANTITY: 10

LENGTH: 15 MIN

WHO: INTERNAL STAKEHOLDERS & PATIENTS

LOCATION: CLINIC

"Preparation is critical. We recommend just going in with three to five questions," Hoggs said as he put down the marker. "These should be at a high level, like, 'What do you think about our fill-in-the-blank service line?' 'What frustrations do you have with it?' You don't want to get into the details at this point. This is not the time to ask where they would prefer the check-in desk. Think strategic questions, not tactical ones. We're trying to understand directionally if our hypothesis is worth pursuing. Each of the questions should be worded to prove or disprove it."

Luigi continued, "Just to clarify, internal stakeholders are people who work for our organization. They have complaints about how we do things, and if we can address them with our new service, that is a tremendous help. We certainly don't want to add any burden. It also promotes the date we are rolling out the final service. We need to make sure that we're not just paying lip service but that we are listening. This is done by summarizing the findings and distributing them back to the employees you interviewed."

"Patients actually referred to two groups of people, the actual patients themselves and their caregivers," Suki warned. "A lot of people forget that most patients have a loved one in their lives who helps them with their healthcare. What that person does can range anywhere on the curves for time and complexity. During the initial interviews, the patient alone is usually fine, but for the deeper interviews, we find it beneficial if they can bring a caregiver with them if they have a higher risk score."

"The most amount of preparation is in finding available patients. For ease of scheduling, we like to find patients who already have an appointment. First, we have to find a clinic willing to participate. Next, we have to find several providers who will allow us to contact their patients. Then, we scour their appointment schedules for patient names. After that, we review the list and then reach out to the patients. We ask them if we can speak to them a few minutes before their appointment or a few minutes after. They will usually tell us which is more convenient for them. We like to schedule more than we need, because there are inevitably cancellations. It really puts us behind schedule if we have to do it an additional day." Georgina continued to read her text verbatim.

"We find it easiest if we have at least two people to conduct the interviews. Ideally, we like to use four total, two in each interview and then just do the interviews back to back. We can get together between interviews and see if we need to make any adjustments to the scripts or questions. Generally, about halfway through we are starting to see some themes and need to make sure that we are staying on track with what we came to look for.

Ideally, we like to schedule this over one day or two days. It's a lot of work, but we like to keep it as short as possible. Once the interviews are completed, we have several hours' worth of audio. Depending on how the information is transcribed, it can take days or weeks for a final copy of the complete transcripts."

"Her content is good, even if the delivery is a little clunky and the text is a bit long," the coach noted.

Georgina cued Hoggs that she was done. The team had started to doze off a bit. He jumped back up to the whiteboard.

"OK, next!"

Deeper Dive

QUANTITY: 10 OR MORE

LENGTH: 45–60 MINUTES

WHO: INTERNAL STAKEHOLDERS & PATIENTS

LOCATION: PATIENT'S PREFERENCE

"This can be a new round of people, or you can reschedule with the same people that you spoke to during the initial interviews. Due to the length of the conversation, we prefer to do it at the interviewee's location of preference. We have done this in every type of place you can imagine," Suki explained.

Luigi spoke next.

"One word of caution: The more public the environment, the worse the recording is due to background noise, so we would recommend that you at least pick an environment with low ambient noise and where you won't be a distraction to others around you. Only conduct this stage after you have done the distillation of the first stage. There is no way to create an accurate script or set of questions without doing analysis and reflection on the first round. Those fifteen-minute conversations should create more questions than answers. Those are the questions that you want to dig down deep into in this round."

Silence. The team looked at each other.

"Your turn, Suki," Luigi said.

"I thought we were trying to make this conversational. You just spoke for a minute," she jabbed back.

"I'll fix it," he replied as he made a note.

Suki looked at her notes and read.

"Having a conversation is far more important in this stage than in the last one. Despite the resource requirement, we like to have two people at these. We only like to have one person talking, but there is a tendency to be script-focused. The second person can jot down notes and hand them to the interviewee requesting additional insights."

Georgina stood up for her next part.

"For this, we like the patient to give as many real-world examples as possible. We don't like them to randomly recount thoughts. There's always a chance to ask why or why not several consecutive times in a row to try to drill down to the root issue. Remember that listening is the key for this as well. However, you have a slightly sharper focus than the last time, so you want to minimize generalities."

Hoggs gave the pen to Suki. "You do the next one."

Immersion

Walking in Patient's Shoes

QUANTITY: 5 OR MORE

LENGTH: UNDER 60 MINUTES

WHO: PATIENT/CAREGIVER

LOCATION: PATIENT'S HOME

"Social workers and home care nurses are familiar with this environment, but very few people in the healthcare system have actually been to patient homes," Suki began. "It was extremely eye-opening for me as a physician. I know many years ago doctors used to do home visits, but never in my career. Just going into someone's house gives you so many insights about them: how clean they are, how much money they have, what type of food they eat and what medications they have."

"We can answer questions like, How many people live there? Do they have pets? Are they in a house, an apartment, a high-rise? Do they own vehicles or take public transportation?" Luigi added. "You can have a good understanding for their personal safety both inside and outside of the home."

Hoggs stood up.

"Typically, the patients who allow us to visit their homes are fairly outgoing and friendly. They like having people over. While it would be nice for us to bring the entire team, we like to respect their space. Keep it to three people or fewer. Sometimes there isn't space for four people."

"Are we supposed to stand up now?" Suki asked after two of the team members had done so.

"They can," Luigi said laughing, "but I'm not. I hate working out."

Luigi wasn't the most active of the team members. He chose to maintain his weight with a balanced diet and avoid the gym when possible.

"Have it your way. I'm joining them," Suki said as she stood up.

"To do an in-person visit at their place of residence, we like to be fairly broad in what data we are going to gather. It's OK for everybody to ask questions, but every person should take their own notes. We're accustomed to one person taking notes, but here it would be inconvenient for us to discuss what is being written down. We will pull the notes together at a summary session immediately afterwards. We don't record in their house and we don't create transcriptions of the dialogue. We're more interested in what social determinants of health may be impacting them. This can vary wildly by ZIP Code, so we make sure that we are visiting patients associated with the clinic in that area. Our service may have to offer a slightly different version for the various clinics. Hopefully, this is accounted for in our personas."

Hoggs stood up and walked back and forth, holding a sheet of paper on which he had written "Distillation." Apparently, this was Luigi's cue to start the next section.

Distillation

"This part is all about: What did we learn?" Luigi said, trying not to laugh at Hoggs's runway walk. "I don't think we have ever had anyone outside of our team read the entire transcription for our stakeholder and patient interviews. Nobody has time for that. We do. We have to. If we did the transcription ourselves, our familiarity is fairly high. However, if someone else transcribed for us, we need to read or listen to it more times. The first time just gets us comfortable with the conversation. We prefer not to take any notes the first time through. The second time we read it through, we highlight sections, comments or quotes that stand out to us."

Suki got up and stood in front of Luigi.

"It's critical for us to extract the gems buried inside hours of interviews, and prep is crucial. We like to have the entire project team prepare their own notes. We like to have our team session less than a week after the available transcriptions. This gives people time to do the work but not feel too rushed," she read, before she walked back to her chair.

The team was getting into this. Their playful culture was showing through a simple reading.

Hoggs went olde English for his next lines.

"When we doeth get together, the conversation hath extremely richness. We goeth around the room, describing what parts stoodeth out to the throng of us and thus partake in a conversation about each. Someone verily summarizes said portions we hath aforementionedly dicussed," he said, before bowing to the audience.

The team laughed and wondered what would happen next.

Georgina stood up and took on a stage theater mode.

"At the end we may have thirty or more areas that are intriguing. That is still too many bullet points for us to be able to simply summarize this stage," she said, dramatically pausing and emphasizing certain words. She continued her antics and moved her hands about demonstrably.

"We try to pull out five to ten salient points that can accurately describe the entire sentiment. We make sure that we keep the stakeholder and patient summaries separate. One is in our self-interest and the other is in the patient's interests. Ultimately, the patient's interest is our interest."

The team clapped, but was shushed as Luigi reminded them he had one more line to read.

"We like to create an additional graphic that serves as a touch point for inspiration. We create a word cloud of the entire transcription. We focus on the top fifty to one hundred words used. If our bullet points aren't aligning with this word cloud, we know we missed something." He concluded this section and attempted to restart the applause. They weren't going to give him the satisfaction.

"Fine!" He leapt from his seat and darted to the whiteboard, grabbing three markers. He removed all three caps and wrote with them simultaneously. His letters took up the whole board.

"Personas!" he exclaimed as he pirouetted back to his seat.

The team clapped.

Personas

That was just enough for them. They didn't need to keep going like this. Without instruction, they settled back into their chairs and read their notes. Georgina began.

"We create segment representatives. One of the things you may find while creating the summary is that there are different points represented. Some patients may be saying very different statements from another.

For example, when we were asking what was most important to them, some patients would mention convenience, while others would mention the relationship with a physician. When that happens, we are discovering different segments with different needs."

"You may have people who are more time-conscious versus people who are more financially conscious. We like to refer to these segments as personas," Suki noted off-script.

Hoggs waited for her to finish before beginning his next part.

"Personas are not created through a brainstorming technique of a team imagining what someone would be like." The coach wanted to make this point clear. He had seen this portion done poorly countless times. "They are created from the distillation of the interviews. You are creating a summarized version of what actual patients are saying. There is a very high likelihood that all of your patients can be lumped into one of the personas identified. These factually-based, fictional characters become one of your most powerful tools for driving your final solutions. After two rounds of interviews and on-site immersion into the patients' lives, you have a better understanding than anyone else. Your personas should reflect this."

Hoggs looked at Suki to see if she had anything to add. She obliged.

"We like to have fun with it. We find a picture of someone who could represent the person and come up with a color theme. We pick out quotes that support that persona, and find several things that each persona would be interested in. It could be sewing, kayaking, children or whatever."

"It's important to make them bigger than life, so we dedicate a section of the wall in our project room to personas," Georgina said, wanting to add a comment too. "They stay there for the entire length of the project. It allows us to always go back to what the patient wants."

"Can I go now?" Luigi joked. "I have a long line and I'd like to get through it."

They nodded. He waited a few long seconds to see if they would say anything, looking at them. They laughed and he began.

"When we have at least three personas, we know we understand our patient. There's no such thing as a universal patient. They're all unique in some way, but we find generalities that differentiate them. Go through the recordings and pull out the best of what's said. For each main point of the project, we like to have a patient quote that best supports the point we are highlighting. Our summary bullet point is very concise, and having a real quote really drills it home with executives."

"Usually there are two or three quotes that really stand out which we use as standalone statements. We create large graphics for each one of these and put them on bold display on our wall. We share these personas with everybody," Georgina beamed. "They take on lives of their own, driving the project and its solutions."

The coach stood up and made the shape of a large O over his head with his arms.

"Aw, a standing ovation," Suki noted as the coach began to clap.

"Well done," he told the team.

Queue

"A queue is a collection. This collection could be major, like projects, or minor, such as tasks. In fact, queues will develop anywhere a process has a poorly designed step that isn't managing its own demand," the coach began, sketching on the whiteboard. "Queues are bad. They kill productivity."

The team had learned over time that their coach hated waiting more than anything else. It wasn't that he was impatient; he was actually incredibly patient, forcing the team to figure things out for themselves instead of giving them the solution. What he didn't have was acceptance of poorly designed processes that forced waits. He knew simple changes could yield tremendous improvements.

Although the coach didn't work well with Kennedy and his strict view of lean in the development world, there were a few things they vehemently agreed on. This was one of them: Maintaining flow was crucial.

"Queues form by an excess demand of inputs. Sometimes predictably, sometimes not. The larger the queue, the worse the effect."

"Like traffic?""

"Or shopping check-out lines?"

"Yes!" the coach responded emphatically. "Perfect examples!"

He drew the basics of both examples on the whiteboard.

"Think of the interstate, or your favorite grocer," he began. "When they are operating within their operational capacity, things keep moving. Each checkout line, each lane of the interstate can easily handle the amount of shoppers or drivers. As they near their limit, around eighty percent, small anomalies can cause great havoc."

He provided a couple of examples as he added to the drawing.

"Suppose a price is missing and someone has to look it up. Flow stops, frustrating everyone."

"And my whole cart is sitting on the checkout belt behind them and people are switching lines to avoid the wait," Suki added.

"Or if a police officer is on the side of the highway," Luigi interjected.

Everybody moaned. They knew traffic. Their roads were not designed for the demands of the population and workforce of their city. This was the case for many large metropolitan areas, but also for the daycare or school that forced everyone to drop off and pick up at the same time.

"Brake lights for miles!" Hoggs exclaimed.

"It becomes gridlocked. Something that should have taken seconds or minutes now can take hours, depending on the severity."

"Like last week," Georgina noted. She was referring to the wintry-mix storm which had started just before morning rush hour. It was miserable. Commutes were triple or quadruple their normal times, even though the area was familiar with snow and ice.

Another collective groan from the group.

"Or shopping on Sundays or during the months-long Thanksgiving-Christmas-New Year's season, especially for those procrastinator days," Suki noted.

"And that's why I order everything online now," Hoggs said. "I can't handle that madness anymore."

The coach could have taken a major detour and addressed the obvious disruption and its impact on retail, but he chose to move the current conversation along.

"Sitting in traffic or a long cashier line is hard. It takes significantly longer for each person to get through. The process should handle demand. Existing real estate and huge construction costs prevent a number of lanes from being added. Hourly salary and employee shift scheduling are problems for retail."

"In every case, resources are limited despite demand," Sheryl keenly notes.

"They're stuck!" Hoggs said.

"Pun intended, I hope," Luigi added.

"Stuck. Literally and figuratively," the coach said, smiling at both the insight and the humor of the group. "The only way is to eliminate demand. The government can offer incentives like high occupancy lanes for carpooling, and employers can offer flexible schedules. Both distribute the demand, allowing less waiting for some people. However, rarely do they achieve the ideal. In that case, you would have to ban driving or force specific hours for shoppers. Neither are viable options."

"I look forward to the day interstates only accept autonomous vehicles," Georgina said. She could get so much done, not having to drive.

"Yes, technology can help. Changing costs are large and will take time. We will get there," the coach replied, shifting the topic back to the team.

"What queues do we face?"

"Projects," Georgina stated instantly. She was responsible for the portfolio. The team's success had turned on the firehose for ideas from the organization. It was build-up from years of frustration. "Everyone has an idea of how things can be better. They see us as the only way to fix it."

"Excellent," coach said as he wrote *Project Funnel* on the board.

"Project tasks," Luigi added. He wanted to squeeze that in before allowing others to comment on projects.

"Project learning," Hoggs corrected him, focusing on the cultural nuances of wanting to drive learning instead of task completion.

"Correct, Luigi. Good catch, Hoggs," the coach said as he jotted *Individual Project Effort* on the board.

"Now, Georgina." The coach directed his attention to her, knowing the answer before he asked. "Are we free to add resources when we want?"

"Well…" she started, knowing she could request exceptions as needed, but also that her hands felt tied most of the time.

"No," she had to admit. If so, they wouldn't have had a list of seventy-something project ideas, and Hoggs wouldn't have been managing several dozen line items every week on his project. "We can't hire to our demand."

"So, what can you control?" the coach prodded.

"Nothing!" Suki said, agitated.

"It may feel that way, but I guarantee we have easier options than fixing rush hour or holiday shopping woes."

The room was silent. They had no ideas. It was a major pain point for them, and they didn't know how to address it.

"Cull," the coach said, as he wrote it on the board. "We have to dramatically reduce the list." He noticed a couple of people rolling their eyes at his comment.

"This is where I help," he said, understanding their concerns for this seeming impossibility.

The coach set a meeting up with the ELT. He ran through the same examples with them. They understood, laughing as they related to each of them and therapeutically complaining about some. The coach knew they got it. For some reason, executives always suffered from short-term memory loss when it came to this. Not really, but they always were looking to make some excuse for why they were different. He braced for the inevitable as he projected the project list on the screen. It was a file type that allowed everyone in the room to access it and comment simultaneously.

"Here are the list of projects Georgina's team has," he began. "Any insights?" He was ready for the discussion that would follow.

"It's a great list," Jill started. "We should be proud of what we're doing."

"I had no idea we had so many," Marc commented, realizing where the conversation was going.

"It's too many," the coach said, deflating the room somewhat.

"But look at the list; they're all important," Jill noted, seeing many that directly improved operations.

"I've already projected revenue from several of these projects," Richard added, highlighting them on the screen.

"My physicians are waiting for a lot of these," Dr. Bertram said, adding to the quagmire that was forming.

Georgina's face looked flushed. Each comment made her wonder why they had scheduled this meeting. The coach looked unfazed. Was that a smirk on his face? It was almost as if this were exactly what he was expecting. "I sure hope he can handle this," she thought to herself.

"We need some of these for our technology roadmap," Joe chimed in.

"My nurses are looking forward to the rollout of these," Valerie said, and pointed to several.

The coach highlighted the first ten rows before graying out everything below it.

"This is what we have to achieve," he said. "Even still, ten is probably too many."

"There is no way," Richard objected.

"I agree," said Jill. "We need all of these."

"Do you need them as soon as possible or do you need them years and years from now?" the coach asked.

"ASAP!" Jill shot back. "We don't have time to wait."

"Just like you don't have time to wait in traffic," the coach replied.

The comment stung. She understood the point, but Richard continued the argument. "We're not sitting on a highway. We're a large organization with a desperate need to improve our financial situation."

"Queuing theory doesn't care what industry you're in. Math is math. Anything over eighty percent capacity and you risk significant delays. We're over seven hundred percent with this list," the coach said.

"But we need a full funnel of ideas," Joe said.

"Technically, we need one good idea waiting when we're ready to start. Anything extra is adding cars to the road."

"But even a small road can handle more than one car," Richard argued.

"Depending on how nice the road is, how equipped the cars are to handle it, and how others are driving." Coach replied. "Ever been on a deserted back road, stuck behind one person you can't pass? How about a snowy road further south?"

They could all relate to these examples. The coach continued. "You know those little green-red lights used on on-ramps?"

"Yes, I hate them," Richard retorted.

"Me too, but they keep the main road from completely locking up, releasing traffic at a more manageable rate. I'm not saying we have just one project waiting. My point is that's technically all we need. Now, if something happens and that project doesn't work out, we'll need another one. Maybe we finish a project more quickly than we thought, and we can start another. Five, maybe ten, is the max we should be preparing in the ready-to-go queue. I say ready-to-go because this is the official list."

Everyone in the room knew there was the unofficial list with double or triple the number of project ideas. All of them were waiting to be vetted and prepped for inclusion into the official list.

"We have three stages of project ideas: early ideas, ideas in process, and vetted ideas. Each idea requires effort. The further along an idea gets, the more effort is required. Once the idea is ready to be launched as a project, a significant amount of the team's resources will be dedicated to it. The more ideas we have, the less we can focus on the projects we're trying to finish."

Marc looked around the room. He knew what needed to be done. This would be painful. He was hoping the ELT would get it themselves before he had to intervene. He didn't like to take the authoritarian approach, but he wasn't afraid to do so when it was necessary.

"But what about all of these on the list? How do we pick the most important ones? You heard everyone here. We're all arguing why they all need to stay."

"Are any of you meeting with Georgina privately, asking her how your projects are moving along?" the coach asked rhetorically.

Some smiled. Others grimaced sheepishly.

"How much work do you think each of those meetings causes? Sure, she can and does run interference on some, but others she feels compelled to answer."

"Everyone's busy. We all have a million things to do," Joe attacked.

"And some people follow the doctor's advice to get healthy again," the coach responded, acting as the Innovation Physician.

There was a silence in the room.

"So what do we have to do?" Marc asked.

"We have to determine which of these projects are the best for the organization. We're going to do it with a combination of quantitative and qualitative methods," the coach replied, having been waiting for this question from the start of the meeting. "We have this tool we use called a Pugh matrix. First we need to choose criteria."

The coach facilitated so Georgina could more easily participate. It was hard to do both, manage the room and contribute well. He did the same thing that Georgina's team had learned to do. The trick came in the scoring and final decision-making. Inevitably, someone would argue for their project's score being changed, or that the weighting was too high or low for some of the criteria. This is where the qualitative portion was used. The coach had learned that a flat score didn't always work, especially with teams that were new to the tool. The final list frequently had a few errors. However, with some productive dialogue, it would be corrected. Over time, they would get better at creating and weighting criteria as well as scoring options against it. Normally, the coach would have had the team take a stab at eliminating the bottom quarter before doing the Pugh. However, it didn't seem like anyone was budging. They would score them all this time, and learn that it would be easier and faster to do a two-stage culling process. The coach wasn't worried.

It took a while, a couple of hours in fact, to do the scoring and create the sorted list. Two-thirds of the projects still seemed important. Some people argued for a project or two in the lower third, but reason prevailed and the bottom third was eliminated.

"Most executive teams struggle with deleting projects. They always want to keep them on a back-up list," the coach noted as they simply hit the delete button on the file.

"We figured they just stood as distractions," Jill said. "If they aren't good enough now, they may never be good enough."

"You are correct. I applaud everyone for realizing that." The coach wondered if the next third would also be deleted.

The debate was intense. Several projects seemed to stand out above the others. These were clear winners. A few began to fade in popularity and wouldn't make it. However, most stood in the gray area of too-important-to-delete, but not good enough to make the top.

Executives didn't like this next part. They all had a vested interest in their projects and getting them on the final list. Not all would make it. It usually meant losing face. Not in reality, but it felt like it. It certainly meant not getting their way and they didn't get to these positions that way.

"We have six projects that are standouts above the rest. After that, we have several dozen of fairly significant importance," the coach started. Richard and Jill became the most entrenched behind their projects. Dr. Bertram followed, but seemed to be able to acquiesce. Valerie was pushing for the one project she had initiated. Without it, she would seem to have nothing. Joe kept pushing his "mission critical" projects.

"Let's say we go to the store but forget our wallet. They don't accept phone payment. We dig through our car and find a twenty dollar bill. How much can you spend at the store?"

"I would negotiate opening a temporary line of credit," Richard said.

Everyone laughed. He probably would.

"Twenty dollars," Marc said, stating the obvious.

"Right now you have twenty dollars. We have enough to 'buy' these six projects," the coach said, pointing to the top of the list." Your queue can't afford any more. Perhaps some day it can."

"We'll get faster and bigger, but not now," Georgina followed the comment. "It's draining and distracting us. We need to focus."

"Not just your team, but our entire organization," Marc added.

"So what are we going to do about the others?" Jill asked.

"I'm going to have to modify my projections," Richard emphasized.

"We're all going to feel like we're losing something. The truth is, we're currently living a lie," Marc responded.

"If this approach is right, then we would never have delivered everything on time anyway."

That was as stunning an admission as the coach had ever heard. He looked around the room. The faces showed that the ELT knew it was true. Executives don't go down without a fight, and they were all secretly hoping to push their projects once outside of the room. They were all expert firefighters and knew how to marshall short-term resources to get done what they wanted. The truth was, it couldn't work this way anymore. That wasn't teamwork. That didn't drive the organization's priorities.

If this exercise had taught Marc anything, it had showed him how much he needed to do to formalize their strategies and initiatives. They needed to do this everywhere in the organization. Everyone was trying to tackle what they thought was important, and it was often in conflict with another department or person. Choosing the top six projects that would best position them for the future was revealing. It showed some misalignment issues with his staff. It showed him what was important to each person. He held everyone accountable for those priorities. Maybe he needed to adjust a few so they could all row in the same direction, together.

"Your official project queue is six deep," Marc announced.

"What about the others?" Jill and Richard said almost in unison.

Marc looked at the coach. "What do you recommend?"

The coach had seen the passion in the team. He wanted to leave on a high note. He felt that deleting the remainder would put a damper on the entire exercise.

"I tell you what," he began. "Let's add a secondary tab to the spreadsheet. We'll put them there."

The room seemed relieved. He knew they would hope to revisit them again in the future.

"Project ideas are like groceries. They have a shelf life. Some are fresh produce, while others are canned goods."

"That's what I'm afraid of," Joe quipped. "I can't wait or it will be too late."

"Unfortunately, that is the price to pay for flow," the coach answered.

It was clear Joe didn't like this answer, and wasn't hiding his feelings for this outsider who was messing up his plans.

"No project can be added to the queue until one moves forward as an official project or is removed due to expiration. Even these six must be ordered by importance. To make it into the official project queue, an idea would have to be better than every idea on the secondary spreadsheet.

"We can set up governance to review and maintain this list, but it should be less frequent than more frequent." the coach cautioned.

The puzzled looks around the room told the coach he had to explain.

"I've seen too many teams review this list on a monthly or even weekly basis. The truth is, Georgina's team can likely only accept a new project every three months or so. We shouldn't meet more frequently than that," he recommended.

"I'll have my admin set up a quarterly review," Marc said, closing the conversation. "We can revisit the frequency after a few meetings."

"Thank you," Georgina mouthed to Marc.

"Anything else?" Marc asked, standing to indicate the end of the meeting. No one said anything.

"Then we have our marching orders. Let's go do them. If you have a problem, come talk to me."

The team stood up and began to file out. Two ELT members said something to Marc on the way out. Most accepted the plan. Teamwork was hard, but they were committed to working together. They would figure it out.

Pugh Matrix for a Test Clinic

The team needed a way to test their ideas. They could go one of several ways.

Luigi jotted the options on the board.

1. Use existing clinics as is
2. Use the team's clinicians and the associated patient panel
3. Create an all new clinic

There were pros and cons to each option. They created a simplified Pugh Matrix to evaluate the options. Their PE team had taught them to use a PICK Chart, but they found it too restricting with only two axes. The Pugh matrix worked great for lists of three or more with multiple variables.

First they would need to list the decision-making criteria. Luigi opened his dry erase marker and asked the team: "What criteria?"

"Cost," Georgina blurted out. As the team leader, she also had to manage the budget. She never looked forward to pitching the ELT for more money.

"Convenience!" Hoggs stated emphatically, and then went on. "I'm the one who schedules the majority of the test appointments. It's never easy getting doctors to let us try something new. Then we have to get the right appointment types and..."

"Let's stick to criteria. We will rate each option later," Luigi said, stopping Hoggs.

The team wasn't supposed to be favoring a specific solution. The process would get them there. He'd had enough one-on-ones with the coach to know that. He thought about one in particular.

"Everyone jumps to a solution the instant they have a clear problem statement." The coach's voice echoed in his mind. "Healthcare is more guilty than other industries. I think it's because they're taught to listen, process and decide almost immediately. By choosing a single solution and testing it to conclusion, you limit your efforts to a sole option. You need to start thinking in sets of three. Every problem should have at least three solutions. Every option should be subjectively and objectively considered. It should never be done by a single person. There should always be at least two people debating—yes, debating—the merits and demerits of each. An individual, as altruistic as they may be, is going to take their own perspective, rely on their own history and experiences. We need diversity to choose wisely. The richness of the dialogue, the complexity of the discussion, and the simplicity of the solution is almost always better."

"Almost?" Luigi asked.

"One step at a time. Walk before you run. For now, we'll say always. I'll teach you more another time," the coach said.

Ted didn't like the answer, but he trusted the coach.

"What other criteria?" Luigi asked the group.

"Speed," stated Sheryl.

"Explain," Luigi responded.

"How fast can we get it up and running?" she replied. She was thinking about all of the hoops they would have to jump through for each, particularly the all-new version.

"How about if I write *Lead Time*?" Luigi asked.

Sheryl thought for a moment and then said, "Sure," just as another member said the same thing.

"Jinx on a Coke!" Hoggs shouted just a millisecond before Sheryl could get it out.

"I was first," Hoggs stated. "I'll take one now."

"No way," Sheryl argued back. "I was."

The team was laughing at the two and egging them on by stating differing opinions.

"Buy us all a drink!" one said.

"Yeah, both of you owe us all."

In most environments, this would have been considered unprofessional and the leader would have stopped the group. Not here. Playfulness was a core value. Early on, there was some heavy pushback from those with offices around the team. They didn't like the noise they made. Many questioned whether they did any work. Sure, they had to make some adjustments so as not to distract others, but they had to disrupt their culture too if they were going to move forward. Georgina made a mental note to include an entire section on culture.

The laughter died down, and Luigi wrote *Lead Time* on the board.

"Anything else?" Luigi prodded.

"I was wondering what we could use to judge the impact of our project. Maybe something like 'testability,'" Sheryl chimed in.

"Go on," Luigi said.

"I mean, if we test something in one clinic versus another versus a repeat, if there's any variation or problem with one over another," Sheryl explained.

"I'm going to write *Authenticity*, Luigi stated, imagining they could make each similar. He caught himself getting ahead and told himself to stop.

He asked for more criteria. The team discussed a few other options, but a Pugh worked best with about five criteria. Above that and you should use a different tool. He was happy with four.

"OK, let me list the options here," Luigi said as he wrote down column one. "And the criteria here," he added as he wrote across the top row, forming a 4×4 table (see page 79).

He could score the table several ways, each having its own pros and cons. The team had done a Pugh on a Pugh, mainly as an exercise, but also to decide which would work best for the team. They would review the method again, but for now would go with the legacy choice. They would use a simple high/medium/low (HML) scoring in each box and then total each. They decided against weighting the importance of each criterium, as the math rarely deviated from the group's intuitive score. If there was a tie, they would compare each against the other using an assumed solution. This was Decision Making 101. It became part of how they did things. They always had three options. They always had a few criteria. The team would score and decide.

This process almost always gave a fourth option the group hadn't originally considered. It would be a 1' or a 3B. That option almost always became the winner because it pulled in elements from the other options to create a high-scoring best alternative. Georgina didn't know how many Pugh Matrices they had used in the past couple of years. She remembered doing her first one and thinking it was so clunky. Now it was second nature. She couldn't imagine making decisions without it. There was no way a single option would ever be considered, at any stage of a project.

The team proceeded to score the matrix. Pughs were usually quick. They only had nine boxes to populate and they only disagreed on a few.

The discussion became the most heated when a specific solution was chosen over another and the scoring was close. Initially, the team was swayed by the most persuasive speaker; however, they found that had a tendency to dilute the diversity and cater to a single individual. Your potential as a Prosecuting Attorney was no longer an advantage. The team didn't allow anyone to dominate. Occasionally, when an outsider would come in, clearly with their own agenda and skewing the scoring to their opinion, the team pushed back, correcting the person and explaining why it was a process, not an autocracy. Sometimes, as the leader, Georgina would have to make the decision and everyone was good with that. She was the one responsible for the project. She represented multiple stakeholders. She knew what members of the ELT would say and what they would approve or deny. The team couldn't just generate ideas and say the score said so. It had to be in the context of the business. Every now and then, she would have to defend a "crazy option" to the ELT, vigorously arguing why. She had to limit the amount of times she did that, lest she lose credibility and be unable to effect the change she championed.

"OK, how does Option 1 do in regard to cost?" Luigi asked.

"High," the team said together, at the risk of another jinx discussion. It was scored high not because it was the highest cost, but because it was the lowest cost. That option would require the least amount of money, so it got a High.

"Convenience?"

"Low!" Hoggs shouted. Someone tried to push back, but was quickly silenced by the group.

"He's right." The team nodded in agreement.

They didn't practice unanimous decisions. It wasn't practical. They didn't have time to get everyone to agree. However, they did have one rule: once the team decided, you aligned yourself with that decision. If you left the room and started your own faction, you were reprimanded. In fact, one person had been "released to her previous position" as a result of passive-aggression. The team had to work together and that meant supporting, not destroying efforts. If you differed, you got to argue your point and were acknowledged for it. Then it was time to drop your view when the team decided. It really was the best way.

The team worked through the rest of the matrix. In the end, none of the solutions looked great. However, they had a direction.

PUGH MATRIX

	CRITERIA 1	CRITERIA 2	CRITERIA 3
EXISTING	HIGH	LOW	MED
TEAM'S	HIGH	HIGH	MED
ALL NEW	LOW	HIGH	LOW

"Option 2 it is!" Luigi announced.

Now it was a matter of making it happen. The team never left a meeting without the 3 W's of Who, What and When. Accountability was highly valued here.

Georgina talked to Jill and Dr. Bertram about which of the team's doctor/clinic combo would be the best. Most importantly, they would have to have a provider that was willing to experiment with new methods, techniques and approaches. On top of that, the support staff would also have to be high-functioning and willing to be a part of it as well. Everyone from medical secretaries to site administrators to nursing staff could easily get frustrated with being an on-again, off-again test clinic. That would eventually bubble up to Jill and she would have no choice but to shut it down. Her priority was daily operations, not innovation.

Georgina had requested that Sheryl print out some of the statistics of the different sites and physicians. They included employee survey results as well as patient outcomes, patient satisfaction, length of service, financial margin and others.

The first meeting was deciding what criteria they would use to filter the list from hundreds of options. Jill didn't want to disrupt the sites that had the highest margins. They were the ones making money for the company and she did not want to disrupt that. As much as she would have liked to see the patient experience improve, Dr. Bertram did not want to use providers with low patient satisfaction scores. Both Jill and Dr. Bertram agreed that the patient panel size should be somewhere below the median. They didn't want to overtax those with high numbers of patients and didn't think those with low numbers of patients would have a problem handling the additional workload. Indeed, most of those providers were not fresh out of residency; they were hires from other health systems. The three of them also decided that they would not target providers in the twilight of their career. Although there may be some interested ones, they needed others, with less experience, to approve. They added a few other considerations. Honestly, since it was their first time through, having the three of them agree on which ones to use was more important than which ones they actually used. They could reassess the test clinic after several months and see if they needed to make any adjustments.

Based on the criteria, Sheryl performed some analysis. It narrowed the list from hundreds to a dozen or so potential provider-clinic combinations.

Georgina scheduled a meeting and distributed the results.

They convened a final meeting to finalize the list that they would reach out to.

"The list looks pretty good. There are a couple of clinics on here that surprise me. I wouldn't include these two," Jill said as she pointed to the screen.

That narrowed the list a bit.

"I'm good with asking all of the providers up there except rows six and nine," Bertram added. "I think you should add Dr. Thill and Dr. Shadding."

Jill nodded in agreement.

The whole meeting only took fifteen minutes. Georgina scheduled it to take advantage of everyone being at the same site on that day. Face-to-face was so much faster than back-and-forth emails. She would inform Hoggs immediately afterward so that he could send the email he had drafted for the finalists. They only needed one or two to express interest. Georgina would follow up with a phone call for anyone with questions. She was hoping to have the provider and clinic finalized within four weeks. That gave a little buffer for any familiarization meetings needed before experimentation began.

AHP

The coach began his explanation of the tool. "The analytical hierarchy process was invented by Thomas Saaty in 1980 (Saaty, T. L. *The Analytic*

Hierarchy Process: Planning, Priority Setting, Resource Allocation. New York: McGraw-Hill, 1980.). Although the tool can be quite complex, a simplified version does wonders for trying to assign waiting to a list of six or more options. We have used the AHP to do analysis on over thirty options. It is simply a pair-wise comparison in a round robin tournament format. The simplified version is not overly scientific but it is infinitely better than most methods used an organizations." The coach stopped talking, allowing the team to continue.

"We have found that the AHP is an essential tool when ranking patient needs," Luigi stated matter-of-factly. "Before we had this tool, we actually weren't even ranking needs, let alone determining which ones carried the most weight."

"Let's equate this with an emergent medical issue," Georgina interjected. "If a patient presents in the emergency department with non-arterial lacerations, and I suspect a broken arm and an acute myocardial infarction, job one is to make sure that the heart remains beating. Eventually we will get around to sewing up the cuts and x-raying and setting the bone. As providers, we are trained to triage and focus on the most important issue first.

"Exactly," Hoggs said, finishing the statement without skipping a beat. "The same could be said for customer needs. if we do a bunch of ethnographic research that results in a list of seven to ten things the customer wishes, we should still focus on fixing the most important one first. That should continue until we have addressed all of the issues. As with any with any development, trade-offs will need to be made in light of schedule, investment or timing issues."

"We use AHP as a method to not only rank the issues, but to decide how much waiting for each issue. That extends to the amount of money and time we spend on developing a solution for it," Suki interjected as if the three were choreographed. "I think it would be best if we provided an example. While we were completing the first one, I questioned its value and thought it was a waste of time. But once I saw the results, it was extremely useful. Now, I can't imagine prioritizing without it."

"Why don't we use our research on high-risk patients as an example?" Georgina asked rhetorically.

Luigi ran to the whiteboard. He always liked writing for some reason. Maybe it was because he felt in control or maybe it was because the person writing for this tool was a facilitator more than a participant.

"Let's start with listing the seven needs we identified," Luigi said. He used A, B, C... instead of numbers.

A CONVENIENCE

B COST

C INITIAL SPEED

D RELATIONSHIP

E RECOVERY SPEED

F CONTINUITY

G ANYWHERE ACCESS

"Now we can set up our matrix." Luigi drew the matrix. "As you can imagine, we moved to an electronic version of this as well. This can be done in a spreadsheet or there is a convenient app that does it as well. You can project the app straight to the screen while you're scoring it. It saves a lot of set-up time. Unfortunately, it's only available on Apple devices."

"A note of caution," Georgina said. "You can't include must-haves as a need. For example, 'patient safety.' It will, or should, always win, but in doing so, skews the rest of the numbers. Just agree that you're going to keep the patient safe with any solution and leave it out."

Everyone nodded.

Luigi went on, "Now we can start the actual tool. We will start by comparing A versus B. There are only three possible alternatives for each box. One is a little better than the other, resulting in a one; one is a lot better than the other, resulting in a three; or the two are equal, resulting in no score."

"Remember what our coach said when we learned this?" Suki asked. "'Doing an AHP is like unraveling a roll of toilet paper. It seems like it will last forever, then all of a sudden it's gone.'"

The group laughed. He was exactly right. If there were ten to fifteen items; it could take forty-five to sixty minutes to do one AHP.

"I just remember looking at that one large matrix and we were still on the first row after twenty minutes. I thought we would never get done," Luigi opined.

Another round of laughter from the group started a series of side conversations.

"OK, let's start with A versus B." Luigi corralled the group back in. "Sometimes they were like herding a bunch of cats," he thought to himself, knowing he was guilty of the same thing when he wasn't at the board.

Individuals in the crowd started shouting. It felt like Wall Street.

"A1!" Suki jumped first.

"Equal," countered someone.

"B1!" Hoggs added.

After opening and closing rounds of arguing their respective points, the group settled on accepting a score of B1, meaning that B was slightly more important than A. Luigi wrote it in the first box.

"We need to emphasize that we're not after consensus here; however, we need the group to agree with the score," Luigi said. "At times, it feels like two lawyers going at it on a trial case in a courtroom. Someone is arguing for their score and someone else is arguing for their score. Others will interject their opinions and eventually a score will be resolved."

"And you can't game the system. Once we set a score, we don't revisit it," Hoggs added. "You can't look at all of the scores and then say, hey, can we go back to such-and-such and check it again? That's just people trying to get the score they're hoping for. It's a disservice to the entire team. Each box should be looked at independently of every other one. At the end, the final tally will tell the answer."

"A versus C." Luigi used a raised voice, hoping to move the group forward.

"A3!" the group yelled almost together. There would be no beverage-buying jinx games now. There would be too many of these.

"That was easy," Luigi said as he wrote A3 in the second box.

"A1!" A couple of members shouted the next answer without being prompted.

"Any objections?" Luigi asked.

Team members shook their heads. He wrote A1.

"Make a note," Georgina said, "If you're not paying attention, you're not going to get a voice here. You have to think fast and you have to know why you say what you say. Otherwise, you can take all day."

The team went on until they had completed the matrix. It only took them about fifteen minutes.

ANALYTICAL HIERARCHY PROCESS (AHP)

	A	B	C	D	E	F	G	
A		B1	A3	A1	—	A3	A3	10
B			B1	B3	E1	B1	B3	9
C				C1	E1	—	C1	2
D					E1	F1	D1	1
E						E1	E3	7
F							G1	1
G								1
						SUM		31

Scoring was simple: you just added up all of the numbers behind each letter.

You then totaled all of the letters to get a denominator, and then divided each letter by the total to know its percentage.

You could then translate those percentages to the original list in ranked order.

CONVENIENCE	32 %
COST	29 %
INITIAL SPEED	23 %
RELATIONSHIP	6 %
RECOVERY SPEED	3 %
CONTINUITY	3 %
ANYWHERE ACCESS	3 %

"Based on the scoring, convenience, cost and initial speed stand apart from the others. Those should be the focus for this solution," Luigi concluded.

"I'm a little concerned that relationship didn't get a higher score," Suki noted.

"And I'm surprised continuity wasn't more important," Hoggs commented.

"I think we should do one AHP for each persona and then we will have a better look at what is important to each one," the coach recommended. "Although it can be quite tiresome to complete one, doing an AHP yields great insight and quantitative perspective for each persona. If you're just doing a single perspective, one works."

"Let's do it!" Luigi jumped up to the board, ready to complete another.

"Imagine if we were using a PICK chart; it just wouldn't work," Georgina observed, as the team settled in for the next rounds.

"Yeah," Hoggs said. "We would argue over how difficult things were, not how important they were."

PICK CHART

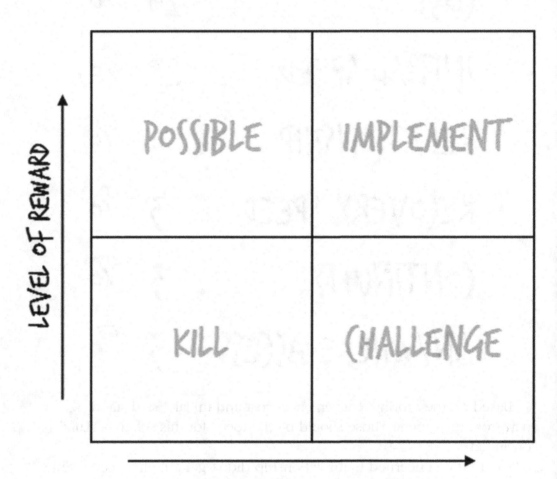

Failure Modes and Effects Analysis (FMEA)

If we have to change something after we launch it, it causes a huge commotion that impacts employees and patients."

The coach had equated this to product quality and warranty failures. One of the tools they used to prevent this was "failure modes and effects analysis," or FMEA. The goal with FMEA was to increase the rate of success by lowering the risk of a failure. The goal was always to achieve 100% performance, but the coach has seen processes that were literally 0% the first time through. Every failure created rework, adding a significant amount of effort to the team to fix. The further down the process went before failing, the more work was required to fix it. This didn't even take into account the impact of making the customer upset. They had learned through monitoring social media that unhappy patients complained far more than content patients bragged.

"I remember the first time we did an FMEA," Georgina said. "A lot of the team members were feeling like it was a waste of time. The coach was going through the first couple of potential failure modes, dragging the team with him."

"I was guilty of being a cynic," Suki admitted. "It had already been a long couple of days and I didn't feel like doing a new exercise."

"We were bumped up right against having to run the experiment soon. We had mapped out the process for the whole thing and didn't feel like flushing out potential failures."

"One of the process steps involved retrieving a form from the printer," Suki recalled. "It seemed like such a basic step, yet the coach pushed us to imagine potential failure modes. I was at my wits' end and remember saying, 'Do we really need to troubleshoot a printer? Shouldn't we be focusing on something else?'"

"Yeah, I remember the coach not letting it go even though the team was pushing to skip it. He reminded us that we were not just trying to fix the process, but to learn the tool as well." Georgina reminisced.

"But we continued to whine, and he relented."

"Wouldn't you know, we went to run the experiment and a printer wasn't working. We didn't have a back-up plan and so we couldn't run the experiment until it was fixed. We ended up having to delay for another week or two."

"If I didn't know any better, I would say the coach sabotaged that printer somehow to make a point."

"Obviously he didn't, but somehow it was like he was looking into a crystal ball."

"From then on, we took our FMEAs very seriously. Honestly, doing them has probably saved us months of time. While you're doing them, it's hard work to develop and implement the counter measures to prevent failures."

"What we have found is that it is always significantly more time to fix them afterwards than it is beforehand."

"We do it once for every experiment and at least one time before we launch, with closer scrutiny on the latter."

"For a lot of us, this isn't the fun part, really pushing the details of the process to make sure that they are robust. We like to look at the big picture and the major things that we are doing. Fortunately, we have a couple of team members now who have become experts with this tool. They love it and they keep us all on track," Georgina said, and pointed at Luigi. "Why don't you share how we use it?"

Luigi walked up to the whiteboard, starting with an explanation as he picked up a marker. "Like the Pugh matrix and QFD, there are a number of versions of FMEA templates out there. The coach always tells us to keep it simple, so we did with this too."

He drew seven boxes, horizontally distributed, on the board. Each one was labeled. The coach smiled, proud of their ability to create it on the fly without the use of a document. That meant that they really knew what they were doing.

FAILURE MODES AND EFFECTS ANALYSIS

PROCESS STEP	POTENTIAL FAILURE MODE	LIKELIHOOD OF FAILURE	IMPACT OF FAILURE	FAILURE ELUDES DETECTION	SCORE	COUNTERMEASURE
		HIGH = 5 MEDIUM = 3 LOW = 1	HIGH = 5 MEDIUM = 3 LOW = 1	HIGH = 5 MEDIUM = 3 LOW = 1	LIKELIHOOD X IMPACT X DETECTION	
		HIGH = 5 MEDIUM = 3 LOW = 1	HIGH = 5 MEDIUM = 3 LOW = 1	HIGH = 5 MEDIUM = 3 LOW = 1	LIKELIHOOD X IMPACT X DETECTION	

Pointing to the first box, Luigi continued.

"Before we can begin, we create a step-by-step outline of the process we are analyzing. The level of detail is equal to the level of potential mistakes. Finer steps mean we can focus on small problems. Large steps mean we usually miss them."

"It took us several runs to determine what level of detail worked for us. We didn't want to create too much work, but we didn't want to miss stuff. As we got more comfortable with the tool, we added detail," Suki said.

"I was the one who took the brunt of the effort," Luigi explained. "I raised my hand to be the scribe, and now I'm the 'expert.'" He airquoted himself with both hands, downplaying his expertise in front of the coach.

"You do a great job," the coach acknowledged, having seen his maturation.

"We usually identify fifteen to twenty-five process steps. Once we have the individual process steps, we can analyze the risk of failure associated with each. The first step is to come up with the possible ways that each step could fail. Each potential failure mode gets its own page of analysis. Eventually, they end up as a row in a spreadsheet. It's not unusual to have fifty or more rows," Luigi explained.

"It may seem like a waste, but we started by handwriting every FMEA on sticky notes and then inputting them into a spreadsheet," Suki explained. "We tried working directly from the spreadsheet, but it was too hard to read and people couldn't focus well enough on the process step we were working on. We didn't rush to figure out a digital tool (to prevent inputting). It was our goal to keep the process and input strong and reliable. Eventually, we created a one-page digital form for each item. Everyone could be in the document simultaneously. It displayed easily and allowed each of us to contribute. Sorry, Luigi, go on." Suki wanted to show that she knew a thing or two about the topic as well.

"Anyway," Luigi joked, "once we have the potential failure mode, we consider it independently. The first step is to score the likelihood of that failure happening. We score it low risk, medium risk or high risk by assigning a respective value of 1, 3 or 5 to it."

"Once we knew the negative impact of a high score, we wanted to push the score values down. Finally we had to just be honest and give the best score we knew. We got better over time," Suki interrupted.

"Next is the score for the Impact of Failure," Luigi continued. "We rate this one based on how bad it would be if that failure occurred. No impact gets a one. Low to medium impact earns a three and high impact failures are assigned a five."

"The last scoring factor is the failure's ability to elude detection. If we know something is failing, when it fails, it has a low rating, or a one. Mediums get a three, and if the failure can happen without anyone seeing it, we assign it a high rating, or a score of five."

"Then, we multiply out each of the risk ratings to get a total," Suki said, unable to help herself. Luigi playfully glared at her until she backed down.

"That score can range from one to one hundred twenty-five. Technically, the cumulative score is called an RPN, and we don't know what that means, so we just call it the Total Score," Luigi said.

The coach mouthed the words "Risk Priority Number," but he didn't care what they called it as long as they did the next step.

"Based on the total score, or risk priority number"—Luigi swelled his chest and spoke formally when he used the proper term—"we have to create countermeasures to prevent them from impacting our process."

"Initially, our scores were so bad we only did things with a score of seventy-five or higher, but then others gave us grief. We ended up settling on addressing any row with a score of fifteen or higher," Suki said, before the entire team told her to be quiet and let Luigi talk. Suki mimed zipping her lips and locking them shut.

"Each high score, as Suki described, forces us to come up with a countermeasure (C/M) to prevent that score from happening. That C/M may focus on any one of the other boxes that contribute to the score. It could be changing the process to minimize the initial failure, or it could be reducing the impact of the failure, or it could be increasing our ability to detect the failure as it is happening. For those with the highest scores, we usually need a countermeasure for each, or what essentially becomes a complete process step revision. It's usually a sign that we didn't design that step properly to begin with. We then rescore those rows with the new countermeasures in place. Once all total scores have been reduced to a nine or lower, we feel comfortable testing it."

Luigi was done. The coach was pleased. They kept it simple and it was a powerful tool. It had prevented a number of major issues in both testing and launch. He didn't like that they still let nines go through, but someday, he knew, they would address those as well.

Tools were just tools without a framework. The team needed a repeatable process in which to use them. They needed a way for a project to go from idea to reality. It was only in that process that the tools would be powerful and their team effective.

Chapter 4

RED Framework

Act of Innovating

"I'm sorry, there is no process that ensures the creative portion of innovating,' the coach told them. "In fact, there are people who can do it and people who can't."

The room was dead silent. You could hear an HVAC fan squeaking somewhere in another part of the building, its noise being carried through the ductwork. There was the low hum of laptop fans.

The coach knew what people were thinking. He had shared this monster concept many times with clients. In his experience, they fell into two camps: one that had to have the process and added people to it, and one that rejected any innovation process, hoping to rely on a couple brilliant people instead. The macro process existed, but when it came down to actual inventing, it took a special skill.

The coach must have reflected on this concept for hundreds of hours. He had to—it was the *one* thing that everybody wanted to know. For years, he would just say some people are better at it than others. It was the truth. It just wasn't the *whole* truth. He didn't know the whole truth.

He was a patent-holding inventor himself. Trained as a mechanical engineer, he'd spent the first decade of his career designing. He'd gotten one patent, so he said he had one. They were just too much work to file, even with a corporate lawyer handling the details. If it had been important, he may have had dozens or over a hundred of them. Not just at work, but at home. Several of his inventions had never been shared outside of his home. His first mechanical invention was to help out his parents when he was just ten years old. They couldn't easily change the light bulb at the top of their stairwell. It was the early eighties, and although there was MTV, there wasn't a low-cost, consumer bulb changer. The bulb was out and needed to be changed. They didn't have a lot of money and didn't have a ladder long enough. He looked around the house. His solution was simple and elegant. He crafted a cone of paper and taped it to the end of a broom handle. He extended his contraption, pressing the bulb into the cone. Wedged tightly inside, it was easy to twist the handle and remove the bulb. Installing was simply doing the reverse. How many people had had that problem and called a handyman to fix it? The solution was in everyone's house.

That was just the first of a long list of things the coach had informally invented. Years later, when he held his first formal job, he was part of the corporate development process. In it, he was forced to be innovative if he wanted to create anything decent. There were thousands of engineers at his Fortune 50 company. They all managed to design their stuff, too. Clearly, some were better than others. He was one of the best.

There he was, deep into another career and getting peppered with the same question: How do you innovate? He should have figured it out years earlier, but to him, it was just do it. He hadn't taken enough time to break down the critical elements. Finally, after several drafts he felt he had it.

"OK, are you ready for this?" the coached asked the anxious group.

Luigi and Hoggs were on the edges of their seats. Process was drilled into these two. If it wasn't process, how could they do it? At the same time, they knew they could do it. They had demonstrated admirable capability on multiple occasions. Georgina held back a stunned look. The coach knew her at this point, and she looked worried. Others were wondering if they could be a part of the team or not.

"How could we get this far in the process and it not be a process?" she was thinking. "Or what if I have assembled the wrong ensemble of players?"

"Tell us!" Luigi blurted out, the wait getting too long for the impatient learner.

The coach took out his dry-erase marker and began to write on the whiteboard.

1. Fact Collection
2. Pattern Recognition
3. Solution Awareness

Leads to...
Creative Hybridization and Metamorphosis

Creative hybridization and Metamorphosis was the cyclotron-like mental process, or what the coach referred to as the "Evolution of the Crazy." "Let's cover each," the coach said.

Fact Collection

You have to understand what's going on and why. It can't be done at arm's length. One has to immerse herself in the problem.

"The biggest error that I see over and over again with people trying to be innovative is to decide too early on a complete solution," the coach started.

"You have to suspend your solution-creating tendencies during this phase. If you have them, you can write them down, but don't dwell on them. You need to get a grasp of the situation. I'm not talking a superficial understanding, I'm talking about a level of familiarity that rivals anyone's on the planet. You need to ask why and how over and over again. One must probe.

"I'm not downplaying solutions here. Some people come up with quite novel solutions before an immersive collection of facts exists. However, they are operating with the belief that their solution addresses the undiscovered issues as well. In fact, it becomes handicap.

"I have been in countless situations where I feel like the fable about the blind men describing the elephant; others are just projecting what they can readily sense, without having the whole picture.

"There should be enough fact collection up front to begin a solid development of the solution. Despite the amount of initial effort, one must continue to reveal additional facts through the other stages of innovating. This will assist in tweaking the solution until its initial launched form.

"Innovators are always collecting facts, pushing aside biases and predispositions to obvious solutions."

"Are you saying we just want to get to the answer?" Luigi asked.

"That's exactly what he's saying," Hoggs answered.

"Personally, I find it a little hard to believe," Luigi countered. "Are you telling me that the majority of solutions are a result of limited fact collection?"

"Not in totality. There are several other steps for an elegant solution to not happen; but yes, it starts here," the coach explained. "It's a combination of impatience and/or arrogance on the part of the designer, thinking they have enough information to fully understand the problem."

You could see the wheels turning in Luigi's head. Both he and Suki appeared to take it a little personally. The coach was not wanting to attack them, but the premise itself and the reality that he saw every day. He could tell, however, that they were not satisfied with this.

"Let's table the discussion for now and revisit it later," the coach suggested.

This was not a tactic to put on the shelf and forget about forever. There was a portion of the whiteboard that kept a small list of topics the team needed to process. It wasn't an official list of things to be done, but a reminder of topics they hadn't come to consensus about. The coach didn't need them fully bought in, but he did need at least a majority that would push in that direction.

He would give them time. They would probably have another debate or two after they left and reflected and then came back together. Honestly, this was exactly the type of approach he was trying to demonstrate. The team would now go out and research both their personal lives and professional examples to prepare for the next conversation.

"Let's move on to the next step, pattern recognition," the coach said.

Pattern Recognition

The coach grabbed the dry-erase marker and wrote on the whiteboard: 1, 2, 4, 8, __, 32? 1, 1, 2, 3, 5, __?

"These are…"

"16 and 8!" Luigi exploded from his seat, interrupting the coach.

"That is correct," the coach said.

"Not all of us studied quantum physics, Luigi," Hoggs said, explaining his tardiness on answering.

Georgina and Suki has solved it but had refrain from shouting out.

"Someone please write Luigi's name on a Post-It note and put a star under it," the coach humorously implored, half-serious.

The team laughed, but Hoggs actually did and handed it to Luigi, who proudly stuck it to his shirt.

"These are patterns in their simplest forms. Basic math makes these easy to solve. Pattern recognition in the complex world of innovating isn't always that simple. The data ingestion forms its own unique algorithm every time, requiring a different mental visualization for each collection of facts.

"What happens when you look for the patterns in multi-axis systems that include the trajectory of consumer electronics, societal values, consumption of time, entertainment, government instability, financial markets and more? Does a pattern predicting the end consumer's needs stand out? What about regional differences? Generational ones?"

The room was silent. They got the math problem, but these examples made their heads spin a little bit. It reminded them both of how far they've come and how far they needed to go.

"Computers can't model this. Not today. Perhaps someday quantum computers with hundreds or thousands of qubits, ingesting the world's data in real-time, can recognize patterns."

"What about artificial intelligence? Isn't that all about pattern recognition?" Hoggs asked, referring to the ever-present AI.

"It is. However, most systems must be trained how to learn. On top of that, they are usually studying in one specific area. They don't cover nearly the breadth of information needed to create products and solutions in this industry or any other," the coach replied.

He was no stranger to this technology. He had dabbled in programming with the available AI tools. There was no such thing as a computer figuring everything out itself. There was still a significant amount of human input and decision-making required. While most of the public had figured that it would replace humans, leading proponents for AI pushed for it to augment humans, not replace them.

"Since the beginning of creativity, it has taken the beauty, complexity, and capability of a human mind. The more complicated the pattern, the more brilliant the mind of the person looking for it must be. We can't all be Russell Crowe's character from *A Beautiful Mind*, but we don't need to be. Simple patterns can be solved by simple people. Complex problems need higher capability. Computers will not be able to do this, at least in our lifetime. We can, however, use this technology, when relevant, to help us be better at pattern recognition."

Big Data Subsection

He didn't want the team to confuse big data and artificial intelligence. Big data was simply the result of a digital information explosion. As the price of storage dropped, people began to store more. Everyone was capturing everything: every industry, both government and private sectors, companies and individuals. Massive server farms were being built around the world to store this data. The same companies that were pushing to make devices and software to collect the data were now scampering to provide storage solutions and analytics for them.

One only had to look at their phone for examples of the clutter created. How many photos of one item did it take to capture its perfect essence?

Burst mode on cameras made it easier to capture the moment, but exponentially increased the amount of data.

The problem was, very few people went back to clean up their own personal data, instead eventually losing it when they switched accounts or their hard drive failed. Now there was the cloud. It was there forever.

Perhaps, one day, there would be "storage wars" for "units of information" that people had long since abandoned. "That would be crazy," thought the coach.

So what was the big difference between big data analytics and artificial intelligence? Entire white papers could be written, but fundamentally it was in the amount of information needed to make predictions. Big data required just that, big data. Analytics would be run on it and patterns would emerge. For artificial intelligence, a limited amount of data was taught to the machine and then the computer could learn from there and identify and predict patterns.

Both were being overused and overhyped. Yes, they were tremendous tools and yielded great insights. For now they were expensive and clunky. Eventually, elegant solutions would exist for both, but not today.

Solution Awareness

"Industries become so self-focused they don't know what's happening in the rest of the world," the coach began. "Most people at least have some exposure to consumer advances, albeit positioned somewhere along the innovation adoption curve."

"Having a view of what's available across humanity at any moment in time is a big plus," Suki interjected.

At one time, their space had only had medical journals and magazines. Today you could have found dozens of magazines across every imaginable area. Suki embraced the broad exploration and became the champion for acquiring physical informational content, eschewing a digital-only, online approach.

"Curiosity feeds this," the coach went on. "Without curiosity, we aren't tempted to search for new things. We get stuck in a rut. We have the same old solutions for the same old issues."

"It really keeps us alert to things going on all around us that we might not even pay attention to," Georgina added.

"Just because another industry is doing something one way, doesn't mean we will do the same thing here," Luigi quipped. "But it helps us think about other ways we could approach something."

The coach was proud of the team for being curious and for truly wanting to know what was happening in the world outside of healthcare. For many leaders, this would have seemed like a distraction. They had enough things they needed to worry about without going outside of their own market niche, let alone their industry.

In fact, in many places he had been, reading magazines was frowned upon during work hours. It meant you didn't have enough work if you didn't have your head down, going at warp speed, all day long, attending half a dozen meetings and responding to two hundred emails. No, his experience reminded him, those workplaces were not conducive to creative thinking and innovation. Sure, people were free to read things off the clock and many people did, but that wasn't the same thing.

If you were indeed going to have broad solution awareness, you needed to ingest as many data points as possible. Maybe someday, one of those data points would surface as a potential solution for a problem you were facing.

"Curiosity means constant learning, constant searching, and constant exploring," Hoggs stated. "The world changes at a rapid pace and new ways to do things surface all the time. We like to be as up-to-date as we can, whether that's pop culture or astronomy."

"It helps us be our best at disrupting our own practices," Luigi transitioned.

"Although we are growing in our technical depth at creating new healthcare delivery models, every project has unique problems and opportunities," Suki tacked onto Luigi's statement.

"Solution awareness doesn't come in a prescribed or predictable manner. It comes from constant exposure to new things and meditating on the problem needing to be solved," the coach added. "In fact, many of these 'eureka moments' come during everyday activities that otherwise seem boring. It's rarely at a desk with a blank computer template in front of you."

This comment prodded the team to chime in with their own experiences.

"Mine always come to me driving home from work," Suki commented. "I think it's one of the first times I slow down enough to reflect."

"An idea will just pop in my mind when I'm doing a workout," Hoggs added.

"Mine come at night when I'm relaxing on my couch at home," Luigi said.

"I can relate to each of those," Georgina agreed with them. "As much as I would like to be able to schedule great solution ideas, they seem to come to me when I'm least expecting it. If I haven't been opening my mind to new things, I find myself leaning towards more traditional solutions. This is certainly the case when I feel rushed."

Heads nodded around the room.

"By increasing our exposure to the world's content, we in fact arm ourselves with a great unconscious tool," the coach transitioned. "And that builds the foundation on which we can evolve it into a truly amazing idea."

Evolution of the Crazy

You couldn't work in isolation on this part. To evolve required heavy feedback loops. What was being thrown at it? What wasn't working? What failed? What were the objections? Others provided this information. Constraints, initially seen as a hindrance, actually became bulwarks for intensely creative solutions. It was seen everywhere in the animal kingdom: camouflage coloring for the chameleon, multiple stomachs for the bovine, chemical "scents" for catfish. All of these traits were perfectly developed for their living conditions. If they didn't have these capabilities, they wouldn't have been able to eat. Survival mandated their biological "features." Creativity made it. Time enabled it.

There are no instant solutions with the absence of repetitive attempts. The shorter the time between the three parts of innovating and the solution, the worse the ultimate solution will be. The longer the time, the better. Organisms have had millions of years. In no company, can a one-hour brainstorming exercise deliver a paradigm shifting solution. An initial idea, maybe. One that takes days, weeks or months to iterate on.

Lexus used to have the tagline "The Relentless Pursuit of Perfection." They knew their first vehicle in 1989 would be a success, but that it wasn't what it could ultimately become. Thirty years later, the newest incarnation can barely trace its roots to that original model. What will the next thirty years bring?

Ideas are only good if they advance the introduction of the final solution. Creating ideas, counting ideas, or asking for ideas are all useless activities if the ability to create something doesn't happen.

It's the evolution of the crazy that results in a public release.

It was in this part that a group of smart people could bounce ideas off of each other. All ideas should start as a virtually impossible dream. Eventually they can be shaped into a reality. Evolving a design from dream to reality requires special skill sets for each stage. Someone with an incredible ability to imagine may completely lack the skills to make it. The person who can make one may not have the capability to regularly deliver it over and over, error-free.

Fortunately, the coach simplified this it into the RED Framework.

RED

The coach was confident in his assessment of development methodologies. He had studied all of them for years and had helped implement versions of each. This man was one of few practitioners who considered the best and worst elements of each and was able to apply that knowledge in real-world experiments with clients.

Whether it was military, government, education, manufacturing, software or non-profit, he had seen it all. Healthcare represented a blank canvas, an opportunity to learn and do it right. There were only a couple dozen "innovation centers" in healthcare. Most of them were focused on medical devices, not care delivery models. There were only a handful doing that. Virtually all of those were tight-lipped about their methods and approaches. They held it as a secret sauce for their health systems' success. Those systems proudly and boldly shared what they offered patients, but they wouldn't let you look under the hood to see how they did it.

The coach saw this as an opportunity to leverage the best of every world and introduce an approach to healthcare that anyone could adopt. He was proud of his effort. With the myriad of innovation frameworks, including design thinking, lean product development, design for six sigma, the scaled agile framework and more, how could the process be so simple as a three-letter acronym? But it was. The coach had assured Georgina that more details would reveal themselves as the team repeated the process, learned, reflected, and adjusted.

The biggest development debate was between stage gate and agile. Stage gate basically referred to any development process with a large, single release that relied on stage gates to progress. Agile represented infinitesimally small releases developed one after the other. Proponents on both sides of the argument had valid reasons why their method was superior to the other. The reality was, Agile was headed in the right direction but had several large gaps that were unaddressed. Eventually, additional constructs plugged the biggest holes, but fundamentally they all had weaknesses.

Methodology Subsection

There were two critical factors in making a decision for a coach and a development methodology. First, he always recommended that clients never choose a coach, consultant or adviser that hasn't actually innovated. The best ones will be individuals who have been through the entire process multiple times, who were the designers and engineers that wrestled over the trade-offs, schedules, cost and needs. Theoretical coaches or those with a function that worked alongside designers don't have the depth you need. There are enough out there that you can find ones who have. It's easy to ask them about their own designs and patents. They should be able to give multiple, quick examples.

As far as methodologies, there are several that can help teams get better. Ultimately, you want to create your own innovation methodology. It should be one that gives you accuracy in meeting needs and speed from idea to launch. It should be cost and resource effective. Simplicity wins. Culture wins. Checklists and templates invariably lose. Don't pick a method because it's the latest or most talked about. Choose one because it addresses the problems you are facing. Not one approach will answer all of your problems. Pick pieces and best practices that develop into your own approach.

Your coach should be versed in multiple methods too. They must serve as the expert in extracting wisdom for your success. Warning signs include intense devotion to one method, bragging about and touting certification, and dismissing others. The best innovation coaches know their limits and humbly admit them. They don't have the answer for everything, but they should serve as the best guide for you to find them.

Looking back, it was a big day for the early team. Their coach had flown in the night before and was there early for the meeting. He would be outlining their framework for innovating and the few people on the team were ready to see what the plan was. Going to the whiteboard, he drew a horizontal line across the board, adding vertical marks at two places, splitting the line into thirds.

He wrote R over the first third of the line, E over the middle section and D over the last section.

"RED?" asked the ever-inquisitive Luigi.

The coach kept writing, ignoring him.

"Research, Exploration, Delivery," he said as he filled in the acronym. "This will fundamentally change your world. I know none of you have a development background. That's OK. In fact, it might be a plus here.

I don't have to retrain you from what you used at random fill-in-the-blank corporation."

Two of the team members were doctors. They were quite familiar with a similar process, the scientific method. RED was all about creating a hypothesis and proving or disproving it.

That was the common ground that allowed Angstrom Health to take the leap of faith with this coach. He couldn't talk about cars or consumer electronics. Healthcare was healthcare. They literally had their own language within a language. The coach had learned long ago that it didn't matter what Toyota or Google did; this highly educated industry did not want to be associated with manufacturing or any other "lesser" business. They didn't work with simple parts on a regulated rhythm determined by predictable demand. There was nothing predictable about demand in healthcare. Of course, you could expect more patients during flu season, or on Mondays, the busiest due to people waiting for the weekend to end, but patients got sick when they got sick. There could be a simple annual checkup for a healthy forty-year-old male followed by a diabetic patient needing an amputation.

The problem was, those companies actually knew how to innovate and healthcare could learn a lot from them. A scientific method based approach like RED could bridge that gap and open the doors for healthcare.

"People get really caught up over how long the RED process can take. It depends on the issue. It could take a month. It could take two years. Let's go back to the overweight patient example. They're not gonna run a marathon in two weeks after a cleanse. It's going to take several months to get them running a 5K or a 10K. From there they can proceed to a half-marathon and then eventually to a marathon. They might be able to do one in a year if they're super dedicated. The RED is the same way. You can do little stuff or you can do big stuff," the Coach explained. "I recommend nothing over twelve months. Just wears on an organization. Executives and team members alike are feeling quite stressed at month thirteen and beyond. The length of the RED framework can be controlled completely through scope, often attached to a technology or a massive training process.

"A couple of ELT members want us to be as fast as possible taking ideas to reality. Apparently, they read some literature about reducing project time by twenty-five to fifty percent," Georgina quipped. "If we say twelve months, they'll ask how long until we can get to nine or six."

"Yes, that request is common." The coach had almost cut her off, knowing what she was going to say, but he waited until she finished her sentence. "My immediate response is, 'How long does it take now?' The funny thing is, very few organizations know. They don't have a formalized methodology that they follow. Every project is run by a different program manager in the way they want to do it and the scope is set at whatever they think can be done, which is often more than they can."

"I get it," Luigi said, pulling from his performance excellence experience, "If you don't have a standard, you don't know how you're performing against it."

"That's right," the coach said. "Look, I can scope any project to make it easy for me to complete it in the time someone is asking for it. Six months? OK. Nine? No problem. But, did I really run one project better than the other one? If there are no standards, you don't know. If you don't have a framework, you can't have a standard, and until you've run through the framework a few times you don't know how well you can perform."

"Someday, we will be able to tell if we can take a twelve-month project and deliver it in nine months, but that is a while off," Georgina said, attempting to summarize.

"Correct," the coach nodded, as everyone's facial expressions reflected their similar understanding of it. "No matter how well you think you know it, the first time or two you go through a process, it's going to be a bit clunky. But then the learning curve will kick in and you will get better. At that point, you will understand what needs to be fixed to increase speed. At some point, you'll hit a wall and then you'll be calling me for help again. If you have a competitive bone in your body, and you compete in three consecutive races, you're going to do whatever you can to be faster in the next one. Eventually, you will need to update your equipment, training plan and coaching to get faster and faster."

"We don't have time for a clunky first time. Richard always like to say we're changing the tires on the car as we drive it," Suki said, throwing down a biggie.

Coach paused for a moment, rubbed his temples and calmly responded.

"Honestly, that is one of the dumbest statements I hear. You can't actually change a flat while driving. You have to stop. The trip hasn't stopped, just the car. Keep driving with a flat tire and soon there won't be a tire. Sparks will be jumping up from your wheel making contact with the road. If you keep going, the wheel will eventually melt and deform until you're no longer able to propel the car forward. I know it's an analogy, but it's a bad one and I don't like it. If you want to get faster, you have to try new stuff, and to try new stuff means you have to build the basics. That doesn't happen in motion. It happens statically. The rest of the organization might be moving forward just like the 'trip' is, But we are paused when we're working through the framework. If we're driving on shredded tire, we have bigger problems than we can fix."

"Some of my proactive diabetics wonder why their A1C levels don't drop as fast as they want them to," Georgina added, equating the analogy to a patient. "A1Cs take time to drop, even when they've made major changes to their diet. You can't instantly get back to good health. It seems like it's the same thing here."

"I couldn't have said it better," the coach remarked. "Let's focus on defining the process and getting through the first time. When, not if, we do this right, we will be adding tremendous value to the organization. Now, I want to give you the key to success for any framework or innovation process."

"Wow, that came out of nowhere," Luigi said as he sat up straighter in his chair. "*The* key?"

"Yes," coach said as the room fell quiet.

He wrote one word on the whiteboard: LEARNING.

"Learning?" Hoggs asked, a bit underwhelmed.

"Learning," the coach stated authoritatively. "And to learn, you have to ask questions and seek information." He began to drift into his Miyagi voice again as this deep truth was revealed. "Always learning. That is key to success," he finished before returning to his normal voice.

"Organizations that learn are ones that get better. When I see a problematic company, I look for what new knowledge they have generated. If they can't provide any, I know they're unhealthy."

"Good thing we all love to learn," Luigi interjected as he looked around the room, hoping for nods of agreement.

"Yes. We. Do." Hoggs punctuated Luigi's statement with an exclamation point.

"Well, I hope so," the coach said as he pointed to the blank walls of the room. "We will cover these walls with layer after layer of what we've learned. This room will be too small to visually display the story we create."

That seemed a bit far-fetched, as well as intimidating, as they were sitting in a decent-sized room with a fair amount of wall space. The coach could tell they were taken back.

"And it won't even feel like work. In fact, the first time we run out of space, you'll look at the walls and ask, 'What can we take down? We want to keep it all up,'" the coach said before anyone could object. "People will flock from around the organization to hear the stories you've created on these walls. Executives will call this their favorite room and will love coming here to hear the latest. That will be bittersweet. Because every time they come here, you will have more work to do. We can't just let them in here anytime," the coach added. "We will set up for more times to present to them on a regular basis and we will give 'guided tours' when necessary. The information on these walls will tell a story that some employees can't handle. Not anyone can just come in here."

"That will be a problem," Georgina said. For the past several years they had been pushing an open door policy, trying to share as much information as they could with employees.

"We're not going to make a big deal out of it. There is potential for people to be offended but if we play cool, it won't be that big of a deal. We can bring people in and share some stuff without talking about everything," the coach replied, refusing to back down.

"OK, but we will play it by ear," Georgina reluctantly acquiesced.

"We're not a secret club working on secret projects," the coach said. "However, what I have found is that the information we discover can be earth shattering, particularly as it relates to our performance compared to the market. There is no need to cause undue alarm."

The coach could tell the team didn't really get this. It was something that they would have to try out and eventually they would understand. He remembered an equivalent to his health transformation. There is a workout heart rate and once it is crossed, recovery becomes significantly longer. In fact, you may have to run slower to go faster. It seems counterintuitive, but it was true. He knew it firsthand. The same was true for the information that would fill this room; it was just right to limit access. One step at a time. Not everything about the framework and how to do it was without conflict.

Research

"Think of this as your patient presentation," the coach began. It's all the information you are collecting to make your initial assessment. Patient dialog and description of the chief complaint. It's equivalent to the Subjective and Objective portion of the appointment."

A couple of heads nodded in the room, verifying he had made an initial connection with the providers.

"This part of the project is all about uncovering what we don't know," he continued. "We are heavy in the learning phase. We collect primary and secondary data so that we can have an expert understanding of both the market and patient needs."

Eyes widened and several jotted down notes.

"A significant portion of the fact collection is on the stakeholder and patient interviews. However, there should be a fair amount of attention spent on current organizational performance, market and regulatory trends and competitive analysis."

"We like to focus on ourselves," Georgina said, admitting to the hubris within her organization. "But we know we need to look outward. How do we know where to look?"

"This tends to be a combination of intentional and accidental discovery. You collect information in whatever areas you think may be relevant. Once you have conducted analysis, a certain area may stand out and require you to do more research there."

That made sense to them.

"Will you give us a list of things to look for?" Hoggs asked.

"A lot of people just want a standard template of what to look up," the coach responded. "I struggle in doing that because I feel like that comes with asking questions. Ask the first question and get an answer. This will cause you to have another question."

"Where do we start?" Hoggs pressed.

"You can always start with the performance metrics your organization uses. Understand why the scores are the way they are. What is the data telling you? What additional insight would help arm your team with the right information to choose the best direction for the next solution?"

"What would be easiest for us?" Hoggs questioned again. Clients liked clear direction, but at some point, the coach had to let go of their hand.

"I always tell teams to start with secondary data," coach explained as he started to cover the details. "There is a lot of information out there that explains what's going on right now. There is no reason to start digging into details until you know the big picture."

"Like what?" Luigi asked.

"Internally, it could be relatively simple things like knowing your active patient roster, or it could be more difficult things like calculating the actual costs to deliver a specific type of care.

"That would be powerful. I don't think we even know if patients are staying in their network or which appointment types we are losing money on," Georgina surmised.

The coach could see the wheels in her head turning, but before she could continue her train of thought he continued.

"Or externally, like what both traditional and new competitors are doing and how they are performing."

"We talk a lot about Saint Agnes Health and how superior they have been, but I have no idea which direction their financials are headed or how their outcomes are," Georgina deadpanned.

"They may seem like they're doing great because they have an excellent marketing team, but there's a lot of published information out there that you could use to put two and two together," the coach added. "Look, you have an entire data warehouse full of information on yourselves. Start looking there."

"So if it exists already and we feel it's relevant, we should collect it?" Hoggs asked.

"Exactly. The key to this part of the framework is curiosity. If you don't have it, you won't get what you need." Their coach hammered the point home, "Curiosity is the foundation for a culture of learning. Period. If you're not curious, learning is absent or forced. If forced, you're learning just to check some boxes. You have to learn to see the patterns. In the patterns, you'll identify the needs and then create unique solutions. Curiosity first, middle, and last."

"I have to admit," Georgina thought out loud, "it will make hiring decisions a whole lot easier. If you're not curious, you're not on our team."

"Good thing I got on when I did," Hoggs whispered.

"Yeah right, you're always discovering new apps, reading articles and keeping us on our feet," Suki countered. Hoggs, like the rest of the team, was highly curious.

Georgina's children were all adults, but not yet making her a grandmother, so the coach asked Suki, the mother of a preschooler, the next question.

"What thing do kids do that demonstrates a desire to learn?"

"Ask questions!" Luigi blurted out before Suki could respond.

"A million of them. Non-stop!" Hoggs added.

"Yes," Suki smiled and nodded at the two single guys who did not have children of their own but had nephews and nieces.

The three of them were constantly sharing photos and stories of the kids and they could all instantly relate to the incessant inquisitions.

"You must also learn to ask questions," the coach added. "Questions are the vehicle for curiosity to translate into learning. Allow me to elaborate."

He relied heavily on the whiteboard for visual support. It worked well as a communication and teaching tool. The team had initially pushed back on using the whiteboard, pushing to use a laptop and a projector. It just couldn't do what the whiteboard could. They had a conference room that had a SMART board where you could draw electronically, but it was clunky too, and usually had some technical issue keeping it from properly functioning. The whiteboard was king for groups.

"This is the R phase of the project. We are Researching. We can blindly hop from one random topic to another until we suddenly find a good direction to take, or we can start with what we're looking for and let the answers direct us," the coach began his explanation.

"Let's take the example of buying a house," he went on. "What is one of the first questions we need to ask?"

"What asking price can we afford?" Suki interjected, having recently moved into a new home.

"Correct. That is a critical question." The coach wrote it on the board and put a box around it. "Without knowing the answer to that question, we risk looking at a whole bunch of places that aren't in the budget. While it is fun to look at the homes of the rich and famous, it's wasted time for your home."

"Are you saying she's not famous?" Luigi asked.

"Or rich?" Hoggs added.

The coach smirked as Suki mouthed, "I'm neither."

"Back to the budget," the coach said, moving quickly back on topic and choosing a different color marker. "What do we need to research to answer that question?"

"How rich she is," Luigi said. "I'll check her bank account."

"Children, let the coach finish. How many cups of coffee did you have this morning?" Georgina asked rhetorically as she maintained order.

"What is our monthly payment target?" Hoggs said.

"How much do we have for a down payment?" Suki added.

"What term does she have for the mortgage?" Georgina asked.

The coach jotted each down quickly, circling each. Then he drew arrows from each of those to the main question. "Great. There are more inputs we could imagine and we could write them all down, but let's stop here for this example."

He pointed to the circled questions he had labeled *Inputs*. "Once we have the answers to these," he said, before pointing to the question in the box, "then we can answer this one. Each will require research. We have to analyze personal budget, compare banks, consider how long we want to owe, etcetera. Eventually, we will have a number, usually a maximum, that we are willing to spend. Let's say $300,000." He wrote the amount next to the boxed question and labeled it *Output*.

"From here we can answer the next big question."

"Where is she going to live?" Luigi was ready to play the game.

"How cool is the area? How far is it from work? What are the schools like?" Suki rattled off several inputs.

"You got it!" the coach said as he furiously scribbled what was said.

"Output equals Old Town," Suki said, jumping ahead based on her experience.

"Now, did you pick Old Town because you like a place there or did you pick Old Town based on the inputs?" Coach wanted to make sure she wasn't gaming the methodology.

"Honestly, we wanted what was best for us. We initially thought we would be by the Hill, but it was too far to work and the schools were questionable. We didn't formally list input questions, but that's what was important and that's how we ultimately picked an area."

"Good," the coach said, "otherwise you may have been sorry when you moved in."

"We were just thinking that the other day, seeing how bad the traffic was just beyond our exit," Suki commented. "Our commutes are manageable but they could have been a nightmare."

"I'm going to stop the example here, but you can see how you can ask more probing questions each time until you finally choose a place to live and eventually the furniture and placement," the coach concluded.

"So how many questions is enough?" Luigi asked.

"I'll answer with a question my English professor would say to us when we asked how long a paper had to be: 'How wide is a truck?' It depends on what the truck has to carry." The coach let that sink in for a moment before seeing the light bulbs turn on in everyone's head.

"Same thing here. Ask the number of questions to get what you're looking for. I'll tell you what I tell every team. The list is never static and it will feel like you'll never stop adding questions. Eventually you will. Start the list of questions with the obvious ones. Put them in an order where each sequential question requires the previous one to be answered beforehand or nearly beforehand. That will prevent a significant amount of rework."

The coach then switched back to the home search example.

"What if you saw a sectional on sale and had to have it, but you hadn't moved in yet? You're taking a risk that it will even fit the floor plan of the place you pick. Or you'll have to make trade-offs on location or cost just to fit the furniture. That's crazy."

Everyone understood that.

"It's just like the Gemini project when I worked for IS," Hoggs explained. "We thought for sure that the software we chose was going to be the best solution, so we signed a purchase order way early to cash in on the salesperson's discount. What a mess that turned out to be."

"That's a great example," the coach stated. "I'm sure if you were to go back and do it again, using a question tool like this would have had significantly better results."

"Sure would have! It turned out another vender released a superior software package a month or two later, at a lower price. If we hadn't signed that purchase order, we would have changed our mind and eliminated a bunch of headaches that continue to this day."

"I like this a lot," Georgina said. "I know this will really help us."

"Just remember," the coach suggested, "it's not static. Add questions when you need to and take them away when they're no longer relevant. As you learn more, some stuff won't make sense anymore and you'll discover things you hadn't thought about before."

"Research ends with an AHP-prioritized list of patient needs for at least one patient segment," the coach concluded.

Exploration

The coach began to explain the next portion. "Exploration is the equivalent to when labs are taken or imagings are done. It's the Assessment portion of an appointment. These insights lead to the differential diagnosis."

The team understood that.

"This is the part of the project where are you leveraging pattern recognition skills. You've done your research. You've prioritized the patient's needs, and you're ready to determine what the solution will be. However, the solution will be made up of many parts. We refer to each of these parts as features."

"What is a feature?" Luigi asked.

"A feature is an independent service characteristic that can contain one or more component parts. For instance, online scheduling. At the highest level, the patient need was asynchronous, independent scheduling. It was birthed out of the pain point of 'difficulty to schedule appointments.'"

"So that is a feature for the service and we call it 'scheduling appointments' or something like that?" Luigi responded.

"Exactly. And one of the characteristics of the service is that a patient can set up the appointment using the Internet. However, in order to do that, a set of individual components must be assembled—the provider template must be known, there must be a way to extract and write data to the associated day, and there must be a patient portal with a usable interface. These are all high-level components that must be individually figured out in order to deliver the online scheduling future for appointments. Each one must have its own feasibility proven and the details determined. Right now, all we are interested in is determining that 'scheduling appointments' is a feature. The rest will follow later in the exploration phase. Right now, it's important to determine all of the features that will address all of the needs." The coach concluded.

"I think I get it." Luigi said. "But I'll need some help, certainly for the first time through."

The rest of the heads in the room nodded. It seemed a little confusing with the nomenclature and low familiarity but they were willing to try. Although he was a little concerned, the coach moved on. He knew they would pick it up.

Feature Identification

"The creation of a list of rank-ordered features marks the formal beginning of the exploration phase. Features are attributes of a service that patients find important. The inclusion or exclusion of specific features could keep patients in your health system or send them somewhere else."

"I can see that," Hoggs admitted. "All it takes is one thing I like or don't like and I'll pick one thing over another."

"Every feature should be the result of what you discovered during the research phase. Each feature must be tied to one or more of the patient needs you identified. You can make two mistakes with features: creating a feature that doesn't align with a need, and lacking a required feature, resulting in an unaddressed need."

"Makes sense. What's the impact if we mess up?" Hoggs asked?

"The first failure results in a significant amount of work for minimal or no patient impact. In fact, these can often have the opposite effect and frustrate patients." Coach replied.

"We like to practice evolution of the crazy for this. It starts with one session where we try to come up with as many ideas as possible. We mix and match, combine and separate ideas. At the end of the session, we have an initial proposal for our feature list.

"We let that list sit for a period of time that can range from a day to week or more. The importance of this is to allow us to individually process what we came up with, hoping that a better idea will pop into our heads. Those ideas are individually recorded for the second session."

"The second session doesn't usually have a ton of ideas; it's usually just limited to a few. However, we will completely question the original list, pushing everyone to come up with better, stronger ideas."

"During this part of the project, the focus is on having teachers that will not just meet the needs but will differentiate us from our competitors. At this point, we have studied them closely, so we know what they are doing. We have also researched some of the top institutions in the world for solutions they are using. Every market is different, so we are not all using the same things at the same time. We don't reinvent the wheel if we don't have to. It's more important for our solution to be elegant and customized to what our patients are saying than it is to copy what 'the best' are doing," the coach continued.

"At first, we struggled with idol worship, thinking that whatever the top institutions were doing, we had to do. What we found was that they were much more of a test-bed for medical device OEMs and bragging rights. In fact, we tried several of their solutions and they fell completely flat. Those were hard lessons," Georgina added.

Feature Performance

"Just having the right feature isn't enough. It has to perform." Coach noted. "The performance level of your features are what patients use to compare you to your competitors."

"What do you mean?" Georgina asked.

"Let me share a short example for you," Coach continued. "An example of a feature could be 'Short Emergency Room Wait Time.' Patients hate waiting in the ER, so advertising a short wait time is attractive. "Short" is relative, though. To one person, short could mean thirty minutes or five minutes. The actual length of the wait is your feature performance level. Let's say you have done your research and patients would be significantly happier with a fifteen-minute wait time. Your current performance is twenty-five minutes. You do a significant amount of work, implementing new technology, changing workflow, and retraining staff to achieve that 40% reduction of wait time. You proudly launch the new ER service, expecting an influx of new, happy patients. Marketing buys a billboard on an interstate informing patients of your fifteen-minute wait time. The number of patients actually drops. Drops? How? You did the research, you talked to patients, you're giving them what they said they wanted. What went wrong?"

"I don't understand how that could happen?" Georgina interrupted.

The coach lifted his hand and kept sharing.

"One day you're driving the interstate and see the billboard for your new service. The very next billboard is one for your competitor. They are also advertising a short wait time, bragging about 'ER Wait Time: 10 Minutes or Less!' You fly through the stages of grief. 'No way they can do ten minutes or less!' you tell yourself. 'They have to measure it differently.' You give a dozen reasons why it can't be true. By the time you get to your destination, you're angry. You attack them. 'Such nerve putting up a billboard right by ours!' That afternoon, you start questioning yourself. 'What if we had pushed for five minutes instead?' You withdraw emotionally that night, saddened by your miss. You sleep poorly, but in the morning, you've accepted the fact you messed up. You're resolved not to repeat it."

"That would be devastating," Georgina commented. "I can't imagine doing all that work for nothing.

"Just remember, the performance level of the feature is just as important as the feature," the coach concluded."

QFD

"One of the simplest tools we use for capturing features, their correlation to needs and their performance requirements is the Quality Functional Deployment [QFD] tool," Hoggs stated.

"Our coach told us Quality Functional Deployment is a poor translation from its Japanese origin. He said Needs Based Solutions would be a more accurate transliteration," Georgina explained. "There was no use for the complete House of Quality, another term used for QFD. We lopped off the roof, the unzipped radars, the basement, the levels. A bunch of stuff that we didn't need. We may revisit some of those elements in the future, but not now."

"QFD has become one of our foundational elements for project success. We can't imagine not using it. It ties our deep research findings to the solution we intend to develop. It serves as a road map for the project's details," Hoggs continued. "A lot of people who know about QFD are turned off by it or no longer use it. We can't imagine that. It's probably the format."

"The traditional format sucks!" Luigi blurted out. It seemed unprofessional and out of place, but he was right. The team had figured out how to get past it.

"At the beginning, we used a basic version of the template. It was intimidating and cumbersome to populate."

"It wasn't just us. We found executives and visitors were turned off by the format. They felt like they needed a decoder ring or a translator to understand what it was saying."

"It lacked the creative flair and visual appeal we boldly used everywhere else," Suki added.

"Ultimately, we simplified it to something that worked for us while maintaining all of the capabilities of the basic template" Georgina continued.

"We don't like to share our version because we feel others need to figure out what works best for them. We recommend starting with a basic QFD and taking the same journey from there."

Feature Creation

"Depending on the size of the project and the batch size, you could develop online scheduling by itself or as a piece of revamping an entire department. Optimally, you would want to find the maximum benefit to the patient with the minimum disruption to the organization. That determines the balance of your stage gate and agile project," the coach began.

"We have not found it worthwhile to do small features on their own. We'd like to get at least three together in order to make a big enough splash for the patient. We can batch together two or three more for the second release and so on until all of the prioritized needs have been met. This should be done in order of importance. There is one exception and that is when a second feature with a lower priority can be more rapidly developed when combined with another feature of a higher priority than waiting. Think of patient training, EMR changes, staff or provider training and similar situations. If your releases are happening every month or two, you don't want to have to retrain the same people every time," Hoggs commented.

"The focus reach release should be the highest-priority item as the main feature being developed, not the grouping of similar ones lower on the list," coach emphasized.

"In fact, we don't like to approach people again more frequently than six months, with some being twelve months. It's a little counter to agile principles, but we have to focus on the speed of the industry and the impact to provider and staff satisfaction," Suki stated.

"Internally, IS is frequently our bottleneck. We try to align most of our future release timings with theirs. They don't like it when we want something else every month or two. Maybe at some point down the road, but not now."

Feature Testing

"Does it really work?" the coach asked the team. "That's what you want to know from testing. Up to this point, you have a bunch of guesses, hopes and dreams."

"With testing, you find out real quick if something works or not. Problem areas instantly become highlighted and you can get staff, provider and patient feedback easily," Hoggs noted, "but you need to be ready; otherwise your test can end prematurely."

"I remember our first experiment. The coach was pushing us to do a quick FMEA on it," Luigi explained. "We were way behind schedule and we were hoping to make up some time. We rushed the preparation, scheduled everything and ran the experiments. We had to stop almost immediately due to a host of problems."

"Did we even make it past the first two patients?" Luigi asked.

"No," Suki remembered. She was the physician running the experiment on a set of her patients. "The first was so stressful and disruptive that I called an impromptu huddle before the second patient. It turned out to be worse for the second patient than the first. We huddled again and cancelled the rest."

"It was humiliating," Hoggs recalled. "We thought we had done so much prep. The coach warned us, but we didn't want to hear it and did it anyway."

"I think we lost three more weeks getting ready again," Luigi interjected.

"It was a month," Georgina commented. "I had attended an ELT meeting the day after the first experiment, unwilling to share the details despite ELT prompting. I tabled it until the next month's meeting, which fell a day after the second experiment."

"We learned a lot about prep. We spent hundreds of hours over several weeks coordinating patient schedules, clinic availability, experiment training and material readiness, only to have it erased by some significant oversight on our part," Hoggs winced. "We never made that mistake again. I think we overprepared a bit. It was a little wasteful and we had to adjust again afterwards, but we found the sweet spot."

"It was more than we thought. Just like our patients. When we tell diabetics to watch high glycemic index [GI] carbs, they have to really watch out. Almost everything these days has them in it. They have to pay close attention to avoid them," Georgina said, giving the experiment medical context. "We can't go into experiments hoping to avoid problems. It requires that we be proactive and search them out beforehand."

"Not only did that help our experiments run more smoothly, but it gave more predictability to our master schedule," Hoggs added.

"To say that our experiments run smoothly might be a stretch," Suki said, pushing back on Hoggs. "The first round is still quite clunky. Even round two is highly manual, requiring significant team resources."

"That's true. We don't want people to get the impression that running experiments is easy. We just want them to know that it can be very rough if you aren't ready," Georgina commented.

"We draft a prototype process on a single page. At the top, from left to right, should be the process steps from beginning to end," Hoggs explained, going to the whiteboard.

"Each process step should have the following listed in rows underneath them." He took the marker and wrote the following points.

1. Purpose of the step
2. Where step happens
3. Patient involvement?
4. Functional resource(s) needed to complete the step
5. Required medical equipment
6. Ancillary equipment (this includes hardware and/or software)
7. Information needed to complete step
8. Estimated amount of time
9. Number one failure mode to be looking for

"The output for each process step should be the input for the next," Luigi added.

PROTOTYPE PROCESS

	STEP 1	STEP 2	STEP 3	...	STEP X
PURPOSE OF STEP					
WHERE STEP HAPPENS					
PATIENT INVOLVED?					
FUNCTIONAL RESOURCES					
MEDICAL EQUIPMENT					
ANCILLARY EQUIPMENT					
INFORMATION NEEDED					
ESTIMATED TIME					
TOP FAILURE MODE					

"When we set up our experiment, we want to validate that each process step can be conducted and that it is actually solving the pain point the feature had intended to solve," Hoggs stated.

"At the same time, we're looking at the performance level. We don't always hit it in the first round or two, but we want to make sure it appears to be achievable in future rounds. If not, we have to cancel the feature," Luigi said.

"We huddle with all involved parties during and after the experiments. This ensures adherence to the plan and allows us to make any on-the-fly adjustments. We're about learning fast and adapting, without completely changing our experimental intent."

"The number of rounds of experiments depends on our confidence in the new process," Georgina inserted. "I always want to reduce the number for cost, efficiency and speed reasons, but we have to be ready for the next stage."

"Sometimes we do three or four rounds and it takes forever," Suki lamented. "I just feel like we're spinning our wheels. Test. Fix. Retest. Repeat."

"It really comes down to how well we identified the needs, translated them into features and developed a solution that achieves our target results," Hoggs succinctly summarized.

"If we think it's going to take more rounds, we use fake patients before trying with real ones," Suki explained.

"It's really important to have the test clinic figured out and a good working relationship with operations," Georgina added. "There were a couple times we rushed in to the clinic and Jill about wrung my neck for not thinking enough about the impacted teams. Not anymore. Readiness is our motto here."

"Before we get done with this stage, we have to have all of our questions answered and a working prototype validated through actual patient interaction. Operations really should be pretty happy with it also," the coach said, wrapping up the discussion.

Delivery

"Here is where the P, or plan of care gets formally created and transferred to the patient. We are scaling from running a few experiments to having it live in many areas. Our goal is to be ready for a robust launch." Georgina explained. "This stage is all about getting a complete service to market. Processes need to be formalized, people need to be trained, and the former service needs to be sunsetted."

"Delivery is about launching a defect-free product or service." Hoggs added.

"Silicon Valley has perfected continuous rollout. Notice I didn't say continuous improvement," the coach began. "I turn off automatic updates on my phone's apps. There is no discipline to being defect free. Many release versions with known bugs, just to get something out there. They rationalize that they'll fix it with the next update. It's horrible."

"That reminds me of Harley Davidson in the 1970s. My dad had one," Georgina said. "Quality and reliability were so poor, he spent more time fixing the bike than he did riding it."

"Right." the coach replied. "Apps aren't quite that bad, but it's a pain when they don't work right. Frozen screens, lock-ups and repeated tasks are the annoyances. Not to mention changing things just to make it look different, completely changing the way it works."

"Our providers and staff are taxed enough keeping up with forced upgrades and new requirements. We can't give them something that's broken. Dr. Bertram would have a fit," Georgina noted.

"Software development is a bad model to copy. With IS being the driving force behind most healthcare advances, there is a tendency to mimic how software companies do things. Don't do it," the coach stated emphatically.

"We found that there are several areas that need to be resolved for a formal launch.' Georgina commented. "There should be a master document for the entire process. This document is not a whitepaper. It is a single page. There can be additional documents as needed, but you need one page that shows the high-level summary.

"We know the entire process could look very different from how it is done today," Georgina added. "Every area that is new will have a different lead time associated with getting it ready for formal launch. Personnel and facility changes usually take the longest. Those details should be fixed as early as possible so that operations can have those ready in time."

If you are going to establish a new process, it should be done in the least wasteful way. The basic principles of lean are the best place to start. Using this methodology will ensure the highest levels of effectiveness, utilization and impact to the bottom line. Most people are familiar with lean at this point in its history," the coach shared. "However, very few know the wastes of lean, how to create a flow cell and using demand to calculate takt. If these concepts are foreign to you, I suggest you seek additional help. Typically, performance excellence teams will be the most versed in this methodology. However, there are a significant number of outside firms with this subject matter expertise. Lean has been in healthcare for nearly twenty years now so you don't have to find someone who can only talk about widgets or manufacturing lines.

Not xREDx

"Over the years, many clients have argued for something before RED and something after RED, like iREDf. They want to add an idea component on the front end and add a feedback component on the backend," the coach reflected. "It just muddies the waters. Think of those as inputs and outputs of the process. Ideas feed into RED as both new ideas and feedback from the previous process. A new idea could be seen as a new chief complaint. Feedback is like titrating a previously prescribed medication. It's the easiest way to nudge the patient's labs to the desired values. If the plan isn't working, you change it completely and start with a new one, hopefully armed with more information. This is no different than a project that becomes a new service. We can't just create the plan, hand it off to operations and ignore the results. We must always follow up to see if we are having the impact we intended. But it needs to be outside of the project. Unless correcting a mistake, the learning should be applied to future generations or releases of the service."

"Oh, I know this!" Luigi commented. He and the coach had argued at length about this. "This is where waterfall and Agile methods demonstrated why they were arch-enemies at times. Agile would say fix it on the fly as a new release. Create a user story, run the sprints, and push it out as fast as possible. Waterfall would say hold up, batch it with another set of features and release the next version at some point in the future."

"That's correct," the coach stepped in. "In fact, best practice is a combination of the two. It works very well. However, it first requires defining a threshold of acceptable performance. The innovation and operations teams have to agree to performance values during the Delivery phase."

The coach waited to see if Luigi would jump in again. He didn't so the coach continued.

"Triggers must be set for each team. Operations is required to problem solve and fix any issues causing a few percentage points of performance drop. The innovation team will be brought in when it is worse, when it becomes clear something was broken in the design. Rework by the innovation team should be viewed as a failure during the RED process. Countermeasures should be quickly developed after a root cause analysis is conducted. The solution should be accurate and delivered quickly to operations, with even more attention given to robustness."

The coach paused for emphasis. "Items that were annoying but not majorly impacting operations should be addressed as part of Idea Queue Management."

The team fully embraced RED. It became somewhat of a mascot for the team. With the obvious color match, the area was punctuated with bursts of it. There were trinkets and novelties celebrating RED.

MVP Subsection

"Remember the first time we asked if we could launch a prototype service as an MVP?" Suki asked their coach in front of the team.

"I thought he was going to break a vein in his forehead," Luigi poked.

The room broke out in laughter with their coach. He had very strong convictions about a simple concept that the software development community had bastardized.

MVP was short for minimal viable product, a concept introduced in the book *The Lean Startup* by author Eric Reis. The book was a game-changer. The concept was created and birthed out of Silicon Valley and had taken the software development world by storm.

Unfortunately, like a great school game of telephone, what was practiced in the real world, after someone telling someone telling someone, was far from what the author had intended.

"I can still picture that day," Hoggs recalled the coach's response to their request. "No way! Absolutely not! We do not have an MVP!" Hoggs continued, impersonating their coach.

The room exploded with laughter again.

"Why did I say that?" the coach calmly asked, with a smile on his face, knowing he would get the right answer.

"An MVP is a prototype, not a sellable solution," Luigi said in an authoritarian voice.

"And a service stripped of features in the name of speed to market isn't one either," Hoggs added.

"Exactly!" the coach exclaimed.

"It's up to us to test what features and functionality work, and we have to decide what would win in our market with our patients," Suki concluded.

The coach stood and applauded.

"You guys get it. Very few people do. The dominant opinion everywhere I go is to get something to the customer as fast as possible and repeat that again and again, constantly introducing new features and capabilities, in an attempt to get extended customer loyalty."

"Like every app on my cell phone," Georgina interjected. "It seems like they release a new version every week."

"That's so annoying," Luigi said, continuing the conversation. "Every time I go to the App Store there are dozens of apps that need to be updated. I don't have an unlimited data plan and I hate having to learn new functionality all of the time."

"And what do we know about healthcare?" The coach asked, wondering if he would get the response he expected.

"Our patients are slow to adopt changes," Hoggs said.

"Go on."

"I mean, with Facebook, I'm opening the app several times a day, so it's easy for me to quickly get used to what they changed," Hoggs added, "but we barely see most of our patients once a year."

"Except for the worst one percent, even the least healthy patients have about ten appointments a year," Sheryl stated, having recently checked the data.

"Can you imagine changing something for them every month? It just doesn't work," Hoggs said, concluding his thoughts.

"The same goes for providers and support staff," Georgina reminded them. "Every time we come up with something new, we have to retrain everybody who delivers care. I can't imagine anyone wanting us to retrain them even every quarter, let alone every month. The system would shut down."

Everyone nodded their heads and offered verbal agreement.

"Exactly. I'm so proud of you," the coach bragged. "You have to make trade-offs relative to the frequency of training and available features in your industry. This means that we have longer cycles between releases, and that's OK."

"In healthcare, innovation resources are scarce. The number of projects we undertake are limited. We can only create so many services. Both our organization and patients can only absorb so many changes," Georgina added.

"And that requires us to identify the biggest pain points and create the most important features. We have to nail it every time," Luigi finished, with a giant, goofy smile.

That point brought up something very important. Every project was critical. Every project had to deliver. It appeared to leave no room for failing. The coach realized this and moved the conversation forward.

Failing

"So what about failing?" the coach asked.

"Fail fast and fail frequently is BS!" Luigi blurted out in a sing-songy, high-pitched voice.

The team laughed again. The offices around them had to wonder if they had a tank of nitrous oxide in there. It always seemed like they were having a good time.

"Yes, because..." the coach said slowly, waiting for someone to interrupt him.

"The probability of success should increase proportionately with the maturity of the project," Suki eloquently stated.

"Impressive!" the coach boasted.

"The project should never fail, only options and alternatives you discarded along the way," he added. This was counterintuitive to what people interpreted from online articles or even those in distinguished periodicals. For some reason, leaders had gotten to the point where they believed a certain percentage of projects failed. In order for one successful project to make it, they would have to manage a large funnel of ideas. This was a mistake. In fact, it was wrong on several fronts.

An idea for a project should be generated around a heavily researched customer need.

"Don't generate ideas just to say we generated 'X number of ideas.' If ideas aren't tied to projects, just trying to generate and manage them becomes an administrative nightmare. They just clog up the queue," their coach would repeatedly tell them.

"We learned the hard way at first. The ELT was pushing so hard for number of ideas as a metric. We set up the method to collect the ideas and it worked," Suki explained.

"We generated hundreds of ideas. Unfortunately, we didn't do anything with ninety-nine percent of them. And it just made the people who generated the ideas mad because we weren't doing anything about them.

"In that case, we failed hundreds of times."

"But that's not the type of failure that bothered us. It was when we had worked so hard on something or tried something new or ran an experiment we were really excited about, and then it failed. The results just didn't support moving forward. Those times really bummed us out. We had poured so much effort into it, hundreds of hours," Hoggs added.

"We were always trying something different. We regularly challenged the status quo," Luigi said. "Our small group was an outsider inside of our organization. People didn't like us. They didn't want us to succeed. Our former coworkers questioned our work. If we kept doing the same thing, we could never get where we needed to be."

"I don't know how many times we questioned whether we would get fired," Hoggs laughed.

"Or just wanted to quit because nothing seemed to stick," Luigi sighed.

Georgina provided a significant amount of cover for her team. They had tried so hard to have their own culture, and failure helped form it. They had a specific element that was forced to be comfortable with failing. In fact, they had christened their own award for failing. They called it the Nōphy, a play on words for "no trophy." They had collected the parts during their trips to supply stores. Eventually, Luigi cobbled stuff together, spray-painted it gold and showed it to the team.

It was first presented to the group who tried using dry-erase markers on the public windows of the community space in a corporate office building. Building management and security put a quick end to that harmless activity.

"So how do we like to fail?" the coach asked.

"We like to fail most with ideas. The earlier, the better," Georgina chimed in. "Once we've completed testing of the prototype, the probability of the project's success should be very high."

"Throughout the entire course of the project, we have to manage not only the need of our patients, but the expectations of our internal stakeholders. Nothing could sink a project faster than an unhappy ELT member."

She knew, because she was the one who had to face them on a regular basis. If she wasn't meeting with ELT members regularly one-on-one, she would have far more embarrassing moments at the ELT meeting and far fewer successful projects.

Chapter 5

Project Reflections

"OK, so if we were to highlight some of your project learnings, what would they be?" the coach asked the team. He knew that this was the client's least favorite part. They were almost at the documentation finish line and he wanted to see a complete picture for next week's ELT meeting.

"Honestly, that first set of research shocked us. It was almost the opposite of what we were doing," Luigi began. "I felt like we couldn't address everything we discovered. We learned too much and failed to deliver."

"Pet projects!" Suki exclaimed. "I took a vow to do no harm. Pet projects violate that vow."

The team laughed. They knew what she was talking about.

"The importance of operations," Hoggs added. "They make or break a project." He had the scars and successes to prove it.

"I'm going to write 'leadership support.' Without Marc, we would have been sunk." Georgina was impacted the most by this, so it was natural that she brought it up.

"And the coach!" Luigi nearly shouted, slapping him on the back.

"You made it easy," the coach demurred. "Let's add some content to each of those points," he said, drawing attention away from himself.

"Can we please add 'technology?'" Sheryl asked, before letting them move on.

The team couldn't believe they had missed that.

"Of course!" Hoggs responded for the entire team.

They pushed each other for several minutes to make sure they weren't missing anything major. They agreed their list was solid. Now for details.

The Shocker

"Initially, we conducted 120 interviews of patients, staff, and providers. Based on those findings, we had a survey completed by over 1,100 patients, inside and outside of our network."

"We had a deep understanding of what everyone thought of internal medicine."

"There were six distinct segments of patients. We called them personas, but we don't want them to be confused with design thinking or Agile personas. Our personas had months of meetings, interviews, and discussions to create."

"We didn't get a bunch of people in the room who could imagine what a patient could be like," Georgina added. "I listened to a conference speaker talk about creating personas. From what I could gather, they simply gathered a small team and created a persona in less than an hour. I honestly don't know how that could be useful. They're creating a Frankenstein of patients, not highly-researched, distinct segments. It just sets up the rest of the project for failure. Our personas are among our proudest work."

"We don't share that information with anyone outside of our organization, especially those in our region. It gives us a competitive edge, so we guard it closely," Suki concluded.

Physical of the Future

"The annual physical is one of the rare moments when healthcare interacts with the patient. For many patients, this is the only time over the course of a year. We found that a significant number of our patients skip it. On one end, for healthy, young patients, it's not evidence-based practice to have them in every year," Georgina stated. "At the other end, for Medicare patients, we *must* see them every year."

"Physicians wanted to see their patient and were leery of passing them off to an APC. If we didn't see them then, who knew when we would see them?"

"However, only one-third of patients were willing to wait for their own doctor if it meant waiting longer for an appointment," Hoggs explained. "Everyone else wanted the earlier appointment with whomever was available."

"Appointment time was crucial. Patients don't always want the next available appointment, they want the appointment when it works best for them."

"Our doctors' panels average two thousand patients. We're pushing to increase that number to five thousand with our goal set at ten thousand.

There won't be enough physicians in the future to keep the panel size low," Georgina explained.

"Even now, giving the patient the time most convenient for them is difficult. When we double or triple the number of patients for each doc, we have to focus on who sees the actual doc and who doesn't need to," Hoggs added.

"In order for this appointment to be the most effective, we need to make sure the patient summary is excellent and able to be understood instantly with minimal digging. Any provider could see at a glance."

"That really enabled our APCs to handle most of the related appointment load," Josh piped in. "They were ready and excited to broaden their scope of practice. There was some anxiety at first, but that's long since gone."

"It took quite a bit of effort on our part. Our EMR provider couldn't create the summary we wanted and it wasn't on their road map. We had to get a third party to extract and display the data. Unfortunately, this solution requires logging into another screen, but the providers have found it so useful, they're happy to do so. We really need EMR integration with the next release," Sheryl stated.

"We wanted to make sure the entire patient is assessed, not just the physical."

"We used a psychological test from a third party that allowed us to understand the entire mental condition of our patients." Bruce explained. "We didn't like the PHQ-9. With a focus on depression, it didn't touch nearly enough elements. By giving our questionnaire prior to the appointment, we know what to address when the patient shows up. For low-scoring patients, our doctors would meet with a psychologist to discuss the results and steps forward, including a referral, if accepted by the patient."

"Also, we wanted to address everything the patient wanted to discuss, not just a single chief complaint. We were so focused on our health assessment, we didn't always get to what the patient wanted to discuss. They can list three to five issues on their form and I know ahead of time what is important to them," Georgina said.

"One patient was an out-of-state college student that had become substance-dependent. He had dropped out of college and was severely depressed. We were able to get him help. Who knows when he would have been in the office next?" Suki shuddered as she reflected on it.

"Instead of the typical After Visit Summary (AVS), we give the patient their one-page summary sheet. Of highest value are the few follow-up steps, not written in medical jargon, but in language the patient can clearly understand."

"It's way better than what we were doing, but we're not happy with where we are. At least it's a start," Georgina admitted. "It's an MVP for sure. Doing what the patient wants means turning our current internal medicine model on its head. We'll get there, but it'll take some time."

"I can't imagine what everyone else is doing, or not doing," Luigi added. "Consumerism is happening faster than people realize. Fail to change, and you may fail to exist."

"We had to change our clinic hours completely," Suki added. "Everyone works, and it's harder and harder to get a day off. There is tremendous demand on Monday mornings and Fridays. We were traditionally 0800 to 1700 but only scheduling until 1600 p.m. We haven't spread to all clinics yet, but we take appointments as early as 0600 and as late as 1930 now. We also open for a few hours late Sunday afternoon."

"It became our goal to keep patients out of the hospital," Hoggs stated. "In fact, if they never had to visit a hospital, we would be happy."

"It sort of became a mantra for us," Suki finished. "It spawned a whole series of projects where we targeted delivering care anywhere but the hospital, even in some acute situations."

Design Thinking Subsection

"There is a lot of chatter amongst my peers about the effectiveness of design thinking. They wonder why we went through such a massive process. What would you say to other CEOs challenging the work you have done?" Marc asked the team during an unscheduled visit to their office.

"I hope our competitors are doing things like design thinking workshops or hackathons," Georgina stated bluntly. "It may be bad for healthcare, but it's good for us. We learned early on that running a workshop every now and then pales in usefulness compared to what we're doing. I mean, we do the equivalent of design thinking workshops every week. You just can't create and maintain sustainable differentiation by randomly assigning people to a design workshop every now and then. All of the big consulting firms are doing it and I'm sure they're generating good ideas, but for a health system to really make a difference they have to embrace the entire methodology and set up a team to run it from beginning to end. And they have to do it over and over again." She finished her bold statement and looked around the room.

Luigi was dying to say something. He was waiting for her to finish.

"You have to have an entire management system around innovating. A little here or a little there may create some value, but the healthcare system has to own the replacement of obsolete service lines and patient care delivery methods," he added.

Now it was Hoggs's turn to chime in.

"I think it was at least a year before we really started to see how this was going to change our business. It was a major investment setting the team up and getting started. We would never have gotten to where we are, even if we had run thirty design workshops in the same time period," Hoggs said, further reinforcing the message.

"It's the same thing as eating really healthy for a few days every few weeks or months, compared to maintaining a healthy diet all of the time. The person who is consistent is just going to be way better off," Suki noted, thinking about the patient reference once again.

"To be honest, the first project didn't end how it started. It was clunky. We got distracted. There were so many new things. We had uncovered a ton of cool things," Luigi admitted.

"We were all over the place," Hoggs grimaced.

"Yeah, but it taught us a tremendous amount about our org, our patients and the process," Georgina chimed in.

"Was it a failure? Technically, yes, but I see it as a huge win. Without that experience, the following projects afterwards would never have made it."

"One of the worst things we initially faced was pet projects. Once we were formalized and getting some internal attention, a couple of executives saw us as a way to get their ideas done. We pushed back, but a couple were much more adept at working the ELT than we were at stopping it."

"It only took one project to end that practice, though," Luigi reminded everyone. "It was a complete. Epic. Failure." He paused on each word for emphasis.

Pet Projects

It can become an embarrassing spectacle when executives meddle. Jerry was somehow on the ELT but ignored by most of the executives. He ran Public Relations for Angstrom Health, although his self-appointed title made him feel way more important. An industry and area outsider, he was learning healthcare as much as he was learning about his new home city. Mostly he liked to schmooze other executives, government leaders and other VIPs.

No one knew what he really contributed. They had net patient loss despite his marketing efforts. Apparently, billboards along the interstate and an incessant Twitter feed about being patient-centered couldn't keep patients who knew better from experience.

Jerry wasn't a team player, taking credit for most wins and blaming others for failures. He had a nascent marketing team, but wouldn't share the data with anyone. He monitored the gold standard of patient experience, the Press Ganey patient survey results. They received thousands weekly. Sure, they knew their score and how they compared to everyone in their area and the nation, but they didn't know the details. Comments provided the richest form of feedback. Every month there were over a thousand patient comments. The data was overwhelming for his fledgling team. Jerry cherry picked the few comments that supported his direction and presented them to the ELT. Although he had the data, he didn't know the whole picture. He had never set up a team to efficiently process and summarize the comments. It was almost as bad as not having survey results in the first place. With a few targeted quotes, armed with the threat of declining scores, he would force the ELT to support him.

When people questioned him, he would argue random points until the person would give up and he got his way. He was a collaborative anti-body. His path of destruction was wide, yet he managed to hide it from the decision makers.

His list of projects and ideas were as long as anyone else's. No doubt, his list was from the host of VIPs he mingled with. If anyone really knew him, they could see past his bluster and verbose explanations of techniques and topics. Jerry was a corporate con, always trying to climb into notoriety despite having the lowest real performance. He managed high ratings and was considered a close colleague, but his niceness was a front that disappeared immediately when dealing with those below him. If you weren't above him, you were below him; he considered that status for everyone outside of the ELT.

Jerry's idea for patient experience ended in a complete failure, but he had kept pushing the team anyway. New members didn't know the process well enough, and the project leader was distracted with almost daily suggestions from Jerry.

Jerry refused to let the process drive the project. The team couldn't find any data to support him. They tried. Their research was extremely comprehensive. What Jerry was asking for wasn't even in the top twenty things patients wanted. It wasn't the twenty-first, either. They just stopped at the top twenty. His idea could've been 234th. Jerry kept pushing, manipulating Georgina, the project team, and the ELT with superior political skills.

Marc visited the team's project room one day. He was alone with a couple of the innovators and asked about the project. At first, they were giving pat answers, the ones they knew Jerry would want. Marc pushed.

"Is the direction you're taking with your solution consistent with what you researched? Give me an honest answer." Marc said.

The two innovators stared at each other. Not even their project leader was in the room. There was no Georgina and there certainly was no Jerry. After a few seconds of silence, Marc interjected, "Something didn't feel right at the last report out, and I wanted to check it out. That's why I stopped by. You guys are the ones closest to the work and I want to know what you think."

"Well, honestly?"

"Yes, I want the truth."

"Our solution is nowhere near what our customers were telling us," they said sheepishly.

"I figured that. Was Jerry pushing for this one?"

Neither of the innovators responded.

"None of this is going to come back to you. I'm going to talk to Georgina and then I'm going to talk to Jerry. What I want is, what would you do given what you know?" Marc made it easy.

Although it wasn't an interrogation, the innovators broke. It felt like it was a safe space. Marc would ensure it was. They proceeded to give him a download of the project, including all of the detours in rework that were necessary to make Jerry solution fit.

"Thank you for your insights. I will sit down with Georgina."

Marc was furious. What a waste of precious resources. Jerry had side-tracked half of the innovation staff with a silly pet project that was no further along than when it started. Like that seventeen-year-old, three-legged pug with cataracts and dual hip arthritis, this pet needed to be put down, put out of its misery. He wondered if he had to tread lightly. Initially, Jerry was one of Georgina's confidants. However, he had sensed a falling out between the two. Perhaps this was why. He scheduled a meeting with her the next morning. Marc simply asked if Jerry was guiding the project against the process. Georgina didn't want to be a narc, but it had negatively impacted her team. They spoke for thirty minutes behind closed doors. Marc emerged, shook Georgina's hand and left.

That mistake marked the end for Jerry. Marc had had enough of his subversive tactics. There would be no more tail wagging the dog. He was disappointed in himself for not seeing it sooner. In his pursuit of personal fame, he left a mess with the innovation team. Marc could not let this go on. He knew there would be blowback, but he knew what he had to do. Marc acted so quickly, it surprised Georgina.

Jerry was excited to see the meeting invitation from Marc in his inbox. He would use this as an opportunity to push another idea on him. However, it didn't go as he had expected. By the end of the week, the head of HR sent a corporate email letting the organization know that Jerry was "pursuing other opportunities."

Georgina didn't know why they used that wording. Everyone knew he was forced to resign or was fired. Jerry would never have left on his own.

Removing executives was one of the CEO's least favorite jobs. The coach knew this was what separated great leaders from good ones. Good leaders let the problem people stick around, afraid of the consequences of getting rid of them. Great leaders deal with it when it is clearly an issue.

"Marc saw it and acted swiftly, way faster than most of his peers at other health systems," the coach told Georgina.

This was strong leadership and the reason that Angstrom Health was making a great comeback.

Leadership Support

"Just seems so trite of an observation. Certainly no one would think of this one as a surprise. But fundamentally, nothing would have happened without the complete support from Marc," Georgina reflected aloud.

He was an outstanding leader. She had seen many over the years, and this guy was about as rare as what her team had accomplished. She wasn't playing the role of sycophant, she was just confident in her assessment.

She remembered her reading from years ago: "Everything rises and falls on leadership."

"That was so true," she thought. She knew that without his support the project would've been doomed. She had proposed so many special projects in her career that she almost didn't bring this one to the table. Maybe after a career of hearing excuses why something couldn't be done, she just didn't have the patience anymore. It was going to move forward here or elsewhere. Fortunately, the right CEO was now in place here and she didn't have to go elsewhere.

Her recommendation to other health systems that were attempting to do this: If your CEO isn't 100% committed to actively advancing the innovation process, your impact and program longevity will be proportionately reduced.

Operations

There were times when they really struggled with operations about replacing an existing service with a new one. Every time the team was trying to implement something new, operations pushed back, claiming it interfered with their performance.

"Initially, they didn't understand that they were riding a horse and we were offering them a car," Suki stated incredulously.

"They didn't like that we were asking them to try something new when they already have extreme levels of pressure to perform," Georgina bluntly stated. "After some obstinance, Marc had to apply some pressure."

"They aligned pretty quickly," Hoggs said. "It only took a few rounds of experiments, and office chatter was that sites wanted whatever we were working on and it wasn't forced."

"Without the active participation of operations, however, we would be sunk," Georgina continued.

"Our work replaces what is happening today. As much as we would like it to be the flip of a switch, it takes some time," Hoggs explained. "We would have to figure out the launch plan and whether it was team-based, site-based, clinic-based or another way. It was impossible to do everything simultaneously. Ops helped us identify where to start and helped us train the teams in the new way."

"The staffing and floor layout changes take the longest," Georgina stated. "Switching who provides care can take months to staff and train. It's tough for sure. Ditto for how the rooms are sized and arranged. Patients didn't like the labyrinth feel, and nurses walked too much."

"Getting enterprise software ready also took some hurdle clearing," Sheryl added. "We had so many rules in place regarding releases that it really hand-cuffed us. We fixed that but it still takes time."

"Honestly, the testing is the fastest part," Luigi said. "We can control almost all of it. Clinics are cooperating and we do the bulk of the heavy lifting ourselves."

"Plenty of room for improvement," Georgina concluded, remembering her recent conversation with Jill about minimizing any impact on daily demand to as close to zero as possible.

The two met regularly. There was no other way for them to be successful. Of all the ELT members, as COO, Jill was the key.

Coaching

The higher the level of your performance, the better coaching you need. Countless times over her career, Georgina had seen morbidly obese patients walk into their appointment. In the beginning, she would give them detailed nutrition and exercise plans. Over time, she realized that this was too ambitious for her patients. She simply started relying on the phrase, "Stop eating french fries." It was simple to remember and it typically had a trickle-down effect on other areas of the diet. From there, she could have the patient work with a nutritionist or a trainer.

Her professional coach, a consultant, did the same thing for her. At the beginning, he just said, "Just ask questions and listen." For four months, that was all they did. She remembered how she just wanted a set of tools or a template that they could follow. He didn't give them what she was asking for. He knew better.

Technology

There were so many firms clamoring to be a part of healthcare. After all, nearly $3.5T was spent annually on healthcare in the U.S., and everyone wanted a piece of it. In recent years, the latest migration included tech firms. It seemed everyone in Silicon Valley had a silver bullet for healthcare. One tech giant after another made a big announcement for the part they would play. One by one, they failed and quietly exited the scene. Then there were the acquisitions. If they couldn't get in with what they had, maybe they could buy their way in. They ended up killing more good firms than creating useful solutions. There was one fundamental issue they all failed to do: immerse themselves in healthcare. It seemed crazy. The leaders that spoke to the media and posted online seemed to understand healthcare, use the lingo, and offer great visions for the future of healthcare. Apparently, it stopped there. No matter how hard they tried, their final solutions aggravated physicians, nurses, and staff. It made workflow more difficult, it added work, and it failed to deliver sustainable savings or improved outcomes. Most of the solutions that were implemented were forced in by payers. They refused to give full reimbursement unless you were on this system or had this capability. It was a riot, and Georgina laughed at the irony. A bunch of Wall Street darlings and tech firms decided what we needed to fix healthcare. "What a joke!" she thought.

Now, it would be different. Georgina would not accept the solutions that tech firms offered. They would work for her team. They would develop what healthcare needed, not what they thought it needed. Angstrom Health was big enough to be an important account. They could take what they developed and modify it for the rest of the market and make their money that way. To do that, they had to send designers and developers to work with us, just like we did with our patients and providers.

Georgina had several open desks in her new space. Vendors would be welcome guests, working alongside her team.

Conclusion

The team had successfully assembled the how-to document of their journey. It was stored in the cloud, so anyone on the team could access it at any time from anywhere. They had sent a link to Marc before presenting the executive summary to him and the ELT. He had read the executive summary and table of contents prior to the meeting. There were hard copies available for each attendee. It seemed like a waste of paper, but some things were easier to view, flip along, and take notes on in hard copy.

Georgina would be presenting alone this time. When the ELT was fully assembled, Marc introduced her and gave her the floor.

"Please reference your packets. I will only discuss the first page. The rest is reference material that supports and explains it," she began. "Focus your attention on how and what we have achieved with our small but world-class team. Although we felt like we had a really slow start, we learned quickly and produced."

On the left side of the one-pager she had the same three points her team had worked on. She titled it "Lean Design in Healthcare: Starting a Journey to Improve Quality and Process of Care."

- Learn the Basics
- Apply the Tools
- Follow the Framework

Georgina spent several minutes highlighting key elements of each and giving practical examples of how they did it.

"Which, of course, led to our output," she announced, drawing their attention to the right side of the page.

These bullet points seemed like any health system vision statement. The difference was, her team had done it.

- Amazing financial results
- Excellent clinical adoption
- Historical best outcomes
- Multiple patient delighters
- Culture of innovation

This wasn't news to the team members, but seeing the methodology, approach and details was eye opening for all of them. The document was a brilliant piece of work. She concluded her overview.

Marc went around the room.

"I hated doing it, but we meticulously measured every dollar impact. The ROI was as good as any they had ever expected with other projects, projects that were never assessed post-implementation and most certainly hadn't achieved projections," Richard began. "I would love to see a systematic financial assessment tool we could apply for every project."

Georgina smiled. The CFO wanted innovation? Win.

"Honestly, as I reflected on operations, this could fundamentally shift how we deliver work," Jill said. "I feel like we bust our butts everyday to achieve mediocre results. This gives us a path to differentiated performance. I'm not looking forward to the seismic change to our staffing model and all of the headaches associated with it."

The room tensed up a bit.

"But," she emphasized, "it's the direction we have to take. We would never get there without Georgina's team."

Dr. Bertram spoke next. "I have providers asking me how they can get a project started in their office. They saw the results of the pilot projects and want it for themselves. They see it as a tool for fixing physician burnout, so they can practice for years into the future."

"Vendors will line up to develop *for* us," Joe started. "I'm shifting the strategy of our team to drive that position for us."

"We saw some positive movement and we're hopeful for more among our nursing staff. They still seem skeptical, but further results will calm them and they'll be champions soon," Valerie concluded.

Georgina had hoped for more nursing impact. The feedback from a private conversation with Jose echoed in Valerie's statement. She would get on it.

"So how much money are you looking for?" Richard bluntly asked. He was thinking about the budget adjustments he would have to make if Marc said yes to her request.

Georgina took a deep breath before responding. She had mentioned it to Marc and Jill before the meeting, but hadn't had time to bring Richard in the loop.

"We're looking to double the investment in our innovation team," she said, and paused before finishing her sentence. "For at least each of the next three years, provided we achieve our annual performance goals."

Mainly this would be increasing her team size, which would allow them to run more projects simultaneously.

"Our core team would grow to more than forty FTEs in three years." Her dream was to eventually have a team of one hundred or more, like the few, rare health systems had in their innovation practices. This would take her almost halfway to that number. It would be nearly impossible for competitors to keep up. Every area they tackled would stand above everyone else, building momentum until Angstrom Health was synonymous with health in their region.

"That would be the biggest win," Georgina thought to herself. "If patients were thrilled to interact with us while simultaneously achieving top outcomes in the country."

She knew they could do it. Those forty FTEs would be a major boost in achieving a complete retooling of every service line. Keeping them fresh would be part of their effort too. They couldn't afford to be replaced by a disruptor that was far more comfortable with risk than they were. She had proven to the company that they could do it, and now it was about expanding that effort and accelerating their impact.

"Objections?" Marc asked the ELT.

Georgina's team had simply built too much positive momentum for people to disagree. There was a latent excitement in the organization once again. Even Joe and Dr. Bertram knew better than to object. Secretly, they both wished they had Georgina's role. Her team was doing what they have dreamed of doing themselves.

Marc waited and then spoke.

"We are our own patient. This process is our plan of care. It's a marathon, not a sprint. We want wellness and health, not acute fixes."

Georgina smiled at the patient analogy. It was working.

"Doubling in a year is tough. Three consecutive years will be a significant strain. We will monitor the metrics closely and hold everyone accountable.

Add to what you have built, don't let the new team members negatively impact what you've begun. You have the pieces in place. Let's scale up!"

With that, the meeting was over. Everyone stood up. They mingled for quite some time before leaving. Marc felt an air of excitement he hadn't felt in quite some time. He pulled Georgina out and congratulated her.

"Let's go talk to the coach. He waiting in my office," Marc said quietly as the two ducked out of the room. They knew the coach was leaving them now.

Final Reflection

They could have used him more, but the coach pushed for them to jump out of the nest. They didn't feel ready, but he knew they would have to venture out on their own. He would always be available, but he needed them to be independent for a while. He would stay in contact and come back when they were ready for the next stage of evolution.

Since he was leaving after a couple of years of regular presence, the coach sat down with Marc and Georgina for their final debrief. Georgina was the newly minted Chief Innovation Officer and latest ELT member. They hadn't filled the vacancy left after Jerry's departure.

"I have a colleague who runs a health system very similar to ours: same size, same mission, and similar patient population," Marc started, "but he and I don't see eye-to-eye on how we should ensure our survival."

"How so?" the coach probed.

"He dismantled his entire Performance Excellence team and scaled back the fledgling innovation work they were doing. He's focused on RVUs and strategic relationships with vendors."

"How's that working out?" The coach wasn't really asking.

"Just like you would expect. They're hemorrhaging cash. People are wondering how he's still in charge. There are rumors that they will be acquired. Attrition is near record levels. Honestly, I feel he is ramming his ship into an iceberg. They continue to mount major annual losses.

"You might know him." Marc shared the man's name.

Sure enough, the coach had met him about a year ago at a conference where the coach was speaking. The other CEO had introduced himself to the coach after the talk and they had scheduled a formal meeting a few weeks later.

"Yes, we met a couple of times," the coach mentioned, without giving any more information.

"Thoughts?" Marc asked.

"Everyone has a way."

Marc could tell the coach didn't want to discuss it any further. A few moments of introspection went by before Marc broke the silence.

"Why do leaders in my position fail after talking to you?"

"Hubris," the coach answered. "They're too proud to seek or accept advice. All of their ideas are great ones, and no one can convince them otherwise. The team around them fails to proactively contribute. They've been conditioned by the constant Whack-A-Mole techniques used to squash ideas and suggestions."

Marc knew it. The coach just confirmed it. The coach then went on to say what no CEO likes to admit.

"The board has to replace them. There is no room for that in the uncertainty of today. Leaders who excelled in operations don't usually shine in the unknown. They need predictability. That time is over. Get a good COO who understands that nothing is static. Let them run the current business while another team is redefining how things are done."

Marc felt comfortable with his capabilities in that area and had sufficiently demonstrated them to the organization during his tenure, particularly as Georgina's team was launched. He shifted conversation to the positive.

"What one quality should they possess?" Marc asked.

The coach didn't hesitate with his answer.

"They must be visionary," he replied.

This wasn't new. You could pick up a hundred leadership or business books on the topic. However, non-academic healthcare rarely rewarded the visionary. Most of them were lauded after their careers, eventually recognized as pioneers years later.

"You have to be able to imagine a different future, a better one. People need hope. Well-thought-out, succinctly crafted visions provide that. You become the Chief Evangelist to your organization on that vision. You know that better than most people," the coach said.

"I thought I did, but it's good to hear it from someone who sees it all the time. I feel that if I'm not picturing where we could be, then no one is. The pressure from today's work paralyzes our tomorrow-brain," Marc replied humbly.

"I couldn't have said it better myself," the coach added graciously.

"Healthcare is too important to our nation and its future to not be fixed. You guys are demonstrating how to lead and others will follow."

Marc breathed deeply before commenting.

"Health systems should lead regulators and payers, not vice versa."

Marc hadn't thought of that in a long time. They certainly could.

"Although you're just beginning your innovation journey and are relatively immature, there are fewer healthcare organizations than I can count on both hands who have what you have here."

Marc was both delighted and proud to hear that.

"At some point you will work out many of the kinks in your current framework, you will improve on most elements and then you won't know what to do next, but you will have an appetite for it."

Georgina knew what was coming next. As a physician, her patients would eventually see her again. That was life.

"You will need outside counsel once again to advance your capabilities to the next level," he continued.

"I would imagine that might take a couple years. In that time, you'll develop groundbreaking patient care services that will set the standard for the nation. You will have the opportunity to connect with thought leaders in the field. You will be a demonstration point that will receive all types of attention. Use it to fuel your progress. Never look back. Never question failure. You have built a great foundation here."

"We know there is always room to be better," Georgina inserted. She had learned that above everything else. It was the essence of innovation, of lean design. There is always better.

"You have plenty of potential to create something incredible. It was a pleasure helping you. I will always be proud of the work we did here."

Marc thanked the coach as the two stood up and shook hands. Georgina hugged him.

"Until next time," the coach said as he walked out.

Index

Printed in the United States
by Baker & Taylor Publisher Services

Printed in the United States
by Baker & Taylor Publisher Services